SPECTRUM

A colorwork collection

in Palette

by Knit Picks

Photography by John Cranford

Additional text compiled and edited
by Jessica Spiegel

Printed in the United States of America

First Printing, 2019

ISBN 978-1-62767-246-7

Versa Press, Inc.
800-447-7829

www.versapress.com

CONTENTS

Intro to Color Theory

Color is powerful stuff—studies show different colors have the ability to influence our moods, making us inspired or energized or even hungry. The colors we incorporate into our knitwear are no exception, so the process of choosing the colors you'll use for a colorwork project is an important one. Though the science behind color theory can get complex, all you need to make confident color choices is a good grasp of the basics.

PRIMARY

PRIMARY & SECONDARY

PRIMARY, SECONDARY & TERTIARY

The Color Wheel

Any conversation about color begins with the basic color wheel and the three primary colors—red, blue, and yellow. Every color traces its origins to some combination of these three colors.

The colors in between each of the primary colors are called "secondary" and "tertiary" colors. Secondary colors are combinations of two primary colors (such as green, which is a blend of blue and yellow) and tertiary colors are combinations of a secondary color and a primary color (like a teal that comes from mixing green with blue).

Though you may only see a handful of colors on a color wheel, the arrangement of the colors can go a long way toward helping you learn the basics of color relationships.

Opposites Attract vs. Friendly Neighbors

"Opposites attract" doesn't just apply to personality types—that goes for colors, too. Colors positioned opposite each other on the color wheel are known as "complementary colors," and putting them together in one project can result in some unexpected looks that you might love.

When a colorwork project calls for more than two colors, you can still use complementary colors as a starting point by using what are called "split-complementary sets." Start by choosing two complementary shades, and then pick one of the two to "split" into the two colors located on either side of it on the color wheel. These color combinations add a lot of brightness and vibrancy to a color palette, while contributing an extra layer of depth and complexity.

While the idea that opposites attract works well, colors that are neighbors on the color wheel can also create beautiful palettes. These are called "analogous colors," and the resulting palettes tend to be more soothing or calming while still utilizing several shades.

Note that using analogous colors in a complex colorwork pattern can be a little more challenging, as similar shades may make the finished design harder to see. (We'll offer some tips to prevent this in the *How to Experiment with Colors* section.)

One fun way to incorporate a pop of contrast into a selection of analogous shades you love is to add one complementary color that's across the color wheel from your analogous colors to your pattern. For instance, an analogous set of blues and greens could work well with a pop of deep orange or red, or a set of pale yellows and greens could serve as the ideal backdrop for a pop of dark purple.

Color Theory Terminology

Along with the general word "color," you'll likely see other related terms used when discussing yarn selection for colorwork projects: hue, value, tint, shade, and tone. There are subtle and important differences between these terms.

Yarn may not allow for blending colors like paint, but understanding these principles can absolutely help you choose colors for your next colorwork project—especially if you're working on a pattern with lots of colors, like stripes or Fair Isle.

Hue: In the broadest sense of the term, "hue" is used as another word for "color," though technically they're different things. A hue is the name of a color family—red, yellow, green, etc.—and while white and black are colors, they're not actually hues. (In the world of painting, hue actually refers to a pure color—red, yellow, blue—without any white or black added to it.) For our purposes, though, we'll use hue and color roughly interchangeably.

Value: A color's "value" is how light or dark it is. A lighter or darker value can come from the addition of black or white to a hue. (This isn't about brightness, however. That's a color's "intensity.")

Tint: Adding white to a hue is a "tint," which is a lighter version of the original. Think pastel yellow vs. lemon yellow—the former is the tint (i.e. the color with a lighter value) to the latter's hue.

Shade: Adding black to a hue is a "shade," which is a darker version of the original. For example, a deep midnight is a shade of blue (i.e. it has a darker value).

Tone: Adding gray to a hue is a "tone," which makes the resulting color less intense than the original. Tones can have lighter or darker values than the original, and they're often quite pleasing to the eye. Antique rose, for instance, is a lovely muted tone of pink.

Choosing Colors for a Colorwork Project

One of the most important—and most fun—parts of a colorwork project is choosing the colors you'll use to make a designer's pattern all your own. If one of the designer's samples has a color scheme you love, then your color selection task is simple. If not, there are a few ways you can make sure the colors you choose will have the overall look you want—many of which can be done before you knit a single stitch.

It's important to remember that there's really no such thing as "right" or "wrong" color combinations when it comes to knitting—it's a personal decision, based on what colors you like to wear. No matter what colors you choose, however, picking a palette for a garment starts with a few basic steps.

First, identify how many colors are in the pattern and whether one of them can be considered a "main" color. This main color (MC) is usually the one using the most yarn in a project, and the color the garment will (at a distance) appear to be. Even a Fair Isle sweater with an allover colorwork pattern will generally register as the main color—a blue sweater with lots of yellow colorwork, for instance, will still likely look blue with yellow accents.

Next, identify the next-most-prominent color in the pattern (this is easy if there are only two colors!), which is the "first contrast color" (CC1). This color's job is to modify the overall look of the MC, making it look slightly different from a distance. That blue sweater with yellow colorwork, for instance, may look a touch more green from a distance if the yellow CC1 is over the entire garment.

Note that the CC1 doesn't need to be lighter than the MC—it can be a darker color or something from another color family altogether. What matters is that the value of the CC1 is different enough from the MC to not cause the design to disappear (with a value too close to the MC in a similar color family) or "buzz" (with a value too close in a wildly different color family).

Finally, identify any other colors in the pattern in descending order of prominence as "second contrast color" (CC2), "third contrast color" (CC3), and so on. These are known as "pop" colors and offer a little spicy kick to your recipe in the form of contrast.

Many Fair Isle and other stranded colorwork designs have at least one "pop" color, often in the color family opposite the MC's color family on the color wheel. You're not limited to the opposite side of the color wheel for your pops, of course, though it's a good place to start. Again, while the color itself is a personal decision, you'll want to keep the value of all your contrast colors in mind in relation to the MC.

How to Experiment with Colors

Experimenting with color combinations before you cast on is a good idea, and it's pretty easy to do.

A big set of crayons or colored pencils and some graph paper is all you need to start playing with colors and see how they work together in the specific design you're making. Fill in the boxes in the pattern's colorwork design until you've got a combination you like. Then, color larger swatches of those colors to use for comparison against actual yarn colorways.

You can achieve similar results with a spreadsheet program on your computer in a fraction of the time, too, though the color selections are often less varied than pencils or pastels.

One easy way to make sure your color choices offer enough contrast to make your colorwork design show up is to look at them in black and white. Gather all the yarns you're thinking of using in your project, lay them next to one another (with all the potential contrast colors touching the MC, if possible), and snap a photo on your phone. Then, open the photo on your phone and use the basic photo editing to change the image to grayscale or black and white. If every yarn is distinct, chances are good you've got a good level of contrast between the values. If two or more look more or less the same, the values are likely too similar and your colorwork will be subtle (at best) or be muddy (at worst).

When you think you've settled on the colors for your design, there's really no better way to see how the yarns will look together than to make a colorwork swatch. Swatching can also be useful if you know what you want your MC to be but you're having a hard time deciding between two or more CC options. Knitting up a swatch with potential color combinations gives you a chance to see them side by side in real life, making you even more confident in your color choices when you finally cast on for your colorwork project.

Our biggest yarn line, developed specially for colorwork and Fair Isle, is Palette. This fabulous fingering weight wool is available in 150 colors that span the color wheel, complete with oddball colors specifically designed to transition between other colors for sophisticated colorwork.

Pro tip: If you receive the Knit Picks catalog with a Palette color spread, tear out these two pages, cut each ball out, and use that as a color selection mix-and-match set of tiny skeins. You can also order a full Palette Color Card of snips in every color so you can see and play with the colors in person (available on knitpicks.com).

Projects shown to the right can be found in Knit Picks' *Creative Color: 2016 Fair Isle* **collection.**

Stranded Colorwork Basics

Managing Multiple Strands of Yarn

One of the challenging things about colorwork is working with two (or more!) yarns at a time. While you could work with one color at a time, constantly dropping one and picking up the other and then back again, this is a very slow method and one that's more likely to result in frustration.

Keeping your colors organized and finding a way to hold the yarn so that it doesn't twist or get tangled, then, is key to working with multiple colors.

There are several ways knitters do this, and the "right" choice is the one that feels most comfortable to you and that allows you to get the most even tension in your knitting. All of them take some getting used to, so try each method and then spend some time practicing (preferably on a small project or even a swatch) the one you prefer.

You may only see one color in each stitch on the front of a project, but remember that there are as many layers to the fabric as there are strands of yarn. Colorwork garments are extremely warm because of this—they're twice as thick!

Carrying Two Colors in One Hand

If you only feel comfortable as either a "picker" (Continental knitter) or a "thrower" (English knitter), then you may want to hold both strands of yarn in the same hand. Whether you hold the yarn in your left or right hand, it's important to keep the strands separate enough that you don't accidentally "pick" or "throw" the wrong one.

Keep in mind that if the pattern you're working on has significantly more stitches with one color vs. the other, you may need to readjust your tension frequently as you pull from one strand more than the other.

Using a Yarn Guide

If you'd like to stick to carrying the yarn with only one hand but you're having trouble keeping the yarn strands apart, there are tools to help. We recommend a tool called a Yarn Guide (available on our site) that slips over your finger like a ring, halting at or near your first knuckle, with a multi-channel top that keeps each yarn strand in its own pathway. Simply open the latch, lay each strand in its own channel in the Yarn Guide, snap the top shut, and you're ready to go.

Note that you may still need to readjust your tension regularly if one yarn is used more than the other, as is the case when just carrying two yarns in one hand without the Yarn Guide.

HOLDING TWO STRANDS IN ONE HAND

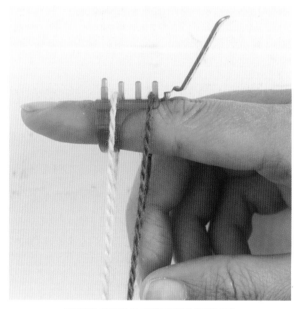

YARN GUIDE GETTING SET UP

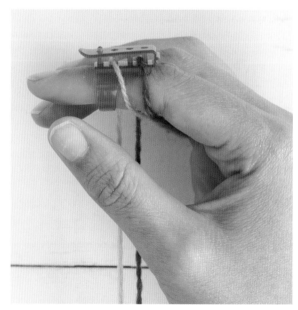

YARN GUIDE IN ACTION

"Scandinavian" Knitting

If you are (or can get) comfortable with either left-hand or right-hand knitting, you may find that holding one strand in each hand is the easiest way to knit colorwork. This method (pictured below), sometimes called "Scandinavian" knitting, is the one endorsed by Elizabeth Zimmerman in *Knitting Without Tears*.

With this technique, it's often easiest to keep one ball of yarn on either side of you while you're knitting, so you'll not only keep the strands in your hands from getting twisted, the yarn balls stay tangle-free, too.

Color Dominance

Along with avoiding tangled yarn, another critical thing to keep in mind is where you're holding your main color (MC) vs. your contrast color (CC). Switching which strand is held to the left or right of the other creates starkly different results in colorwork knitting; this concept is known as "color dominance." The "dominant" color in a pattern is not necessarily the same as your MC—in fact, it usually should be exactly the opposite.

Think of the dominant color as the one creating the design rather than the one creating the background. You want the design to appear as if it's laid over the top of the background color, rather than trying to peek through from underneath. Holding the CC as the dominant color, then, makes sure this is the look you get. Of course, which color you want to be the dominant one is entirely up to you—and since it's actually a pretty fun experiment to try this, switching which color is dominant and which is not, you can try both out on a colorwork swatch before you cast on to see which you prefer.

No matter what you decide, the dominant color should always be held to the left of the nondominant color—whether on one finger, in a Yarn Guide, or in your left hand while the other strand is in your right—and you should keep this consistent throughout the whole project.

Wrapping Floats

To keep the back of your work tidy, you may want to consider securing the longer loose strands, or "floats," by wrapping the two yarns while you're knitting. Most knitters would probably leave shorter floats (with three stitches or less) alone, but floats of five or more stitches may benefit from wrapping.

Keep in mind that wrapped floats may sometimes be visible from the front of the work, so test it both ways before getting too far into a project.

There are two commonly used techniques for wrapping the unused color behind your work while you are knitting your multi-color project. With a little practice, you can master these techniques and they will become indispensable in working with color patterns.

Wrapping Yarn from Your Left Hand

When you come to the stitch you want to wrap, put your working needle into the stitch on the left-hand needle and then also under the yarn strand on the left hand (Photo 1). Next, wrap the right-hand strand of yarn around the working needle to knit it—but before you pull it through, push the left-hand yarn strand back off the working needle (Photo 2) so the only color you knit to create a new stitch is the one from your right hand (Photo 3). You'll see the left-hand yarn strand is wrapped behind that stitch (Photo 4), keeping it tame.

Wrapping Yarn from Your Right Hand

When you come to the stitch you want to wrap, put your working needle into the stitch on the left-hand needle and wrap the yarn from your right hand around the working needle as if to knit it—but don't (Photo 1). Next, start to knit from the yarn in your left hand (Photo 2)—but before you pull the left-hand yarn through, push the right-hand yarn strand back off the working needle (Photo 3) so the only color you knit to create a new stitch is the one from your left hand (Photo 4).

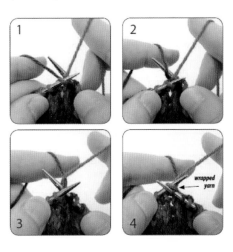

How Often to Wrap Floats

Some knitters like to wrap floats frequently and regularly, while others do so when the floats "feel" too long for their taste. Whichever camp you fall into, note that you must have "normal" (non-wrapped) stitches on either side of every wrapped stitch or the weaving effect won't work. Also note that if you have several rows in a pattern that may require wrapping, don't wrap at the same places in each row—that can make the fabric look strange.

Note: If your stitches are twisted, then you are bringing the yarn through the wrong way.

Yarn Tension in Colorwork

Even if you don't struggle with tension or gauge when knitting with one color, knitting colorwork with multiple strands requires some adjustments.

Holding both strands of yarn too tightly can result in fabric that is taut and puckered. Holding them too loosely can make the fabric look messy. Some knitters go up a needle size (or two or three) just for the colorwork portions of a garment—using US 9 needles on a colorwork yoke of a sweater that's otherwise knit with US 6 needles, for instance. Some simply experiment with how they hold the yarn until they get a fabric they like.

Wrapping floats can help, but even if you're wrapping stitches frequently, you still want to be conscious of carrying the unused colors at the back of the work loosely. Remember, loose stitches or strands can be tightened, but it's virtually impossible to loosen stitches that are too tight.

Nervous about your first colorwork project? Start small! Hats or even can koozies can be excellent beginning projects for stranded colorwork.

Steeking

Knitting takes a great deal of time and dedication, and that's especially true when you're working on something complex like a colorwork garment. Bringing a pair of scissors anywhere near something you've painstakingly knit, then, might seem like a terrible idea.

In fact, "steeking"—putting a panel of additional stitches in the place where you'll later cut the fabric open—is a useful tool in a knitter's arsenal. Not only that, sometimes it's the only way to create the look you're going for.

What a Steek Is & Why You Need One

A "steek" is a small strip of extra stitches added to a garment between two pieces of knitting that will eventually be separated by cutting them apart (like the 5-9 stitches in the middle of a cardigan pattern that don't follow the rest of the design).

Colloquially, many knitters refer to the whole process—knitting the panel, reinforcing the stitches, and cutting fabric open—as "steeking."

Steeking is often used in complicated colorwork patterns so that you don't have to work them flat, eliminating the need to learn to purl while stranding colors—and also reducing the number of yarn ends left over from changing colors. Not only that, knitting a colorwork pattern in the round also keeps the design looking more consistent, as it's common to have different tension when purling vs. knitting.

This method originated with Shetland knitters and traditional Fair Isle colorwork, in which intricate stranded colorwork designs dominate entire garments—including V-necks and cardigans.

But steeking isn't only for colorwork. Even if your garment is a solid color, most people find knitting preferable to purling—so instead of working back and forth, steeking lets you knit the whole tube for the body of a sweater (for example) in one piece before cutting open the holes you'll need to add sleeves or make it a cardigan. This has the added benefit of requiring less seaming.

How to Add a Steek & Cut Your Finished Knits

Adding a Steek Panel

Before you start knitting, decide where you want to add a steek to your project. In that place, you'll want to add 5-9 stitches for the steek (odd numbers are helpful so there's one clear center column of stitches), alternating colors for every stitch. The stranded colors in this area will later help keep the steek from unraveling and will also help maintain your stranding tension evenly over this area.

Reinforcing the Steek

There are three common methods used for reinforcing both sides of where you intend to cut in the steek panel—crochet, hand sewing, and machine sewing. The method you should use is primarily determined by the type of fiber in your fabric.

Crochet Reinforcement

Fibers that are naturally a bit more sticky—such as non-superwash wools—are good candidates for a crochet steek reinforcement. This is also a useful method when the fabric is especially thick.

Use a sturdy, non-superwash wool yarn (slightly lighter weight than the yarn in your garment is best) in a different color than your garment and the appropriate size crochet hook for that yarn.

With the right sides facing you and the reinforcement yarn held behind the work, crochet duplicate sts between two rows of knit stitches, two stitches away from the cut line on both sides of the steek.

- Start by bringing a loop from the back of the work under the cast-on row to the front, leaving a 6" tail.
- Insert the crochet hook between the two stitches from front to back, grabbing the yarn behind the work.
- Pull a loop through the knitted fabric from back to front, and through the loop that's already on the hook.
- Work one crochet loop for every knit row, pulling work snug (but not too tight, lest the fabric pucker).
- Continue in this way up the entire column, creating a crochet chain stitch up one side of the steek panel.
- To finish, use a tapestry needle to run the ends of crocheted chain through the back of itself—be sure to pierce both the back of the crochet stitches as well as the knitted stitches, being careful not to let it show on the front side.
- Repeat this process on the other side of the steek panel.

Hand-Sewn Reinforcement

For more slippery fibers—superwash wool, for example—a crochet reinforcement may not be enough to keep fabric from unraveling after it's cut open. In these cases, sewing is the best option. Sewing by hand is convenient for anyone lacking a sewing machine, and ensures you'll catch every single stitch.

The cut line will be directly in the center of the steek, and your lines of stitching (one stitch to each side of the cut line) will help to stabilize the cut edge.

Hold the work so the steek panel is in the center and the right side is facing you. Make sure to smooth any yarn ends away from the center cut line beforehand (or, better yet, weave them in). Laying it on a flat surface can ease the sewing process.

Use a tapestry needle and a sturdy, non-superwash wool (slightly lighter weight than the yarn in your garment is best) in a different color than your garment.

- Sew a running stitch between the first and second stitches to the right of the center cut line, making sure to catch the floats between every stitch. Sew right through each strand of yarn, not between them.
- Continue in this way up the entire column. When you reach the end, turn the work and repeat the process down the same column you just did—only this time, you'll be backstitching. This means that you'll be working your needle through the yarn in between the first line of stitches you did, creating an overlapping chain that makes the reinforcement twice as strong.
- Be sure you're making tiny stitches, piercing the yarn with every single stitch if possible.
- Don't pull too hard on your stitches, or the fabric of the garment will pucker.
- To finish, snip the end of the yarn, leaving a 6" tail, and weave in the ends.
- Repeat this process on the other side of the steek panel.

Machine-Sewn Reinforcement

The slipperiest fibers—like cotton or alpaca—require machine stitching on a steek panel to make sure they stay where you want them to. The basic concept is the same here as it is for hand sewing (you're sewing through the yarn, not going between stitches as you would with a crochet reinforcement), though you'll be using thread instead of yarn. Again, choose a thread that's a different color than your garment so you can see it more easily.

- Working slowly, machine stitch a line of very small stitches and loose tension on one side of the center cut line in your steek panel, making sure the needle is piercing every stitch.
- You can choose to place the stitches directly next to the cut line—running a line of stitches through the left and right legs of all the stitches on either side of the ladder through which you'll cut—or place it one or two stitches away from the center line. (For added reinforcement, some choose to sew two lines on either side of the cut line.)
- Repeat this process on the other side of the steek panel.

Cutting the Steek

Once you've reinforced the steek panel on both sides of the center cut line, lay the piece on a flat surface and smooth it out.

If you used the crochet reinforcement method, you'll need to gently separate the crochet chains to expose the ladder running up the center cut line. If you used a sewing method, you may find it helpful to mark the center cut line with removable stitch markers or even a loosely-sewn line of thread to make sure you stay in the right column.

In either case, using very sharp scissors (some prefer small scissors for better control), cut each strand of the ladder in the center cut line carefully. Don't forget to cut the floats behind the work, too. Work slowly to prevent cutting something you don't mean to—like the reinforcement stitches you just made.

When all the cutting is complete, you'll be able to open up the fabric, admire your handiwork, and pick up stitches for button bands, V-neck bands, or whatever the pattern calls for.

Some knitters like to sew pieces of grosgrain ribbon over the steeked edges, and others simply tack down the edges with needle and thread. Both options help keep the edges secure and prevent fraying.

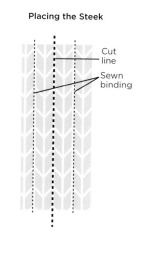

Sewing the Steek

Running Stitch   *Backstitch*

Placing the Steek

Cut line

Sewn binding

DIAMOND MOSAIC COWL

by Jessica Strough

FINISHED MEASUREMENTS
22.5" circumference × 12" height

YARN
Knit Picks Palette™ (fingering weight, 100% Peruvian Highland Wool; 231 yards/50g): MC Wonderland Heather 26044, CC Conch 24557, 1 ball each

NEEDLES
US 2.5 (3mm) 16" circular needles, or size to obtain gauge

NOTIONS
Yarn Needle
Stitch Marker

GAUGE
32 sts and 62 rnds = 4" in Mosaic Stockinette Stitch in the round, blocked (gauge is not crucial, but it will affect finished size and yardage requirements)

For pattern support, contact jstrough88@gmail.com

Diamond Mosaic Cowl

Notes:

Carry just one yarn at a time to create this fun and easy-to-knit mosaic pattern! Pick two colors that speak to you, going for bold high-contrast, muted monochromatic, subtle neutrals, or complementary hues (like the sample).

The Diamond Mosaic Cowl is knit in the round using slipped stitches to create a bold geometric pattern. Because only one strand of yarn is worked at a time, this pattern is great for knitters who are new to colorwork.

The chart is worked in the round; read each chart row from right to left as a RS row.

Always slip stitches purl-wise with yarn in back.

Diamond Mosaic Pattern (in the round over a multiple of 6 sts)
Rnd 1 (using MC): (K1, Sl1, K3, Sl1) to end.
Rnd 2 (using CC): (Sl1, K2) to end.
Rnd 3 (MC): (K2, Sl1, K1, Sl1, K1) to end.
Rnd 4 (CC): (Sl2, K3, Sl1) to end.
Rnd 5 (MC): (K3, Sl1, K2) to end.
Rnd 6 (CC): (K1, Sl2) to end.
Rnd 7 (MC): (Sl1, K5) to end.
Rnd 8 (CC): (K2, Sl3, K1) to end.
Rnd 9 (MC): (Sl2, K3, Sl1) to end.
Rnd 10 (CC): (K3, Sl1, K2) to end.
Rnd 11 (MC): (K1, Sl2) to end.
Rnd 12 (CC): (Sl1, K5) to end.
Rnd 13 (MC): (K2, Sl3, K1) to end.
Rnds 14-18: Rep Rnds 4-8.
Rnds 19-21: Rep Rnds 1-3.
Rnd 22 (CC): (Sl1, K2) to end.
Rnd 23 (MC): (K1, Sl1, K3, Sl1) to end.
Rnd 24 (CC): (K2, Sl3, K1) to end.
Rnd 25 (MC): (Sl1, K5) to end.
Rnd 26 (CC): (K1, Sl2) to end.
Rnd 27 (MC): (K3, Sl1, K2) to end.
Rnd 28 (CC): (Sl2, K3, Sl1) to end.
Rnd 29 (MC): (K2, Sl3, K1) to end.
Rnd 30 (CC): (Sl1, K5) to end.
Rnd 31 (MC): (K1, Sl2) to end.
Rnd 32 (CC): (K3, Sl1, K2) to end.
Rnd 33 (MC): (Sl2, K3, Sl1) to end.
Rnd 34 (CC): (K2, Sl3, K1) to end.
Rnd 35 (MC): (Sl1, K5) to end.
Rnd 36 (CC): (K1, Sl2) to end.
Rnd 37 (MC): (K3, Sl1, K2) to end.
Rnd 38 (CC): (Sl2, K3, Sl1) to end.
Rnd 39 (MC): (K2, Sl1, K1, Sl1, K1) to end.
Rnd 40 (CC): (Sl1, K2) to end.
Rep Rnds 1-40 for pattern.

3x2 Rib (in the round over a multiple of 5 sts)
Rnd 1: (K3, P2) to end.
Rep Rnd 1 for pattern.

DIRECTIONS

CO 180 sts with MC, PM, and join for knitting in the round, being careful not to twist sts.
Work 3x2 Rib until piece measures 1.5″ from CO edge.

Begin working Diamond Mosaic Pattern. (Note: You will be alternating colors every rnd. To help you keep track, the working color for each rnd is indicated in both the written and charted instructions; the non-working color is slipped.)
Cont working pattern until piece measures 10.5″ from CO edge, or desired height, ending on either Rnd 1 or Rnd 21.

Cut CC yarn, leaving a 5″ tail.
Using MC, knit one rnd, then work 3x2 Rib until section measures 1.5″.
BO in pattern.

Finishing

Weave in ends, wash, and block.

Diamond Mosaic Pattern

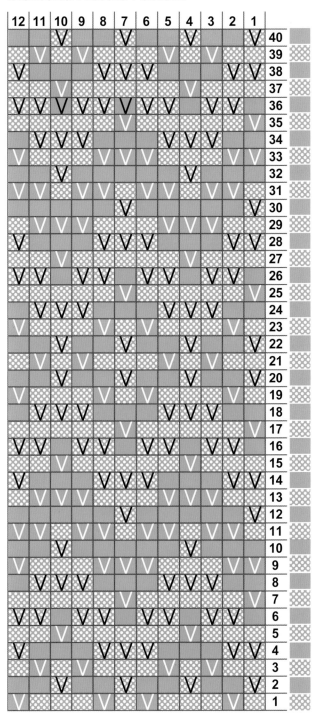

LEGEND

Main Color (Wonderland Heather)

Contrasting Color (Conch)

Knit Stitch

Sl
Slip stitch purl-wise, with yarn in back

The working color for each round is indicated by the box to the right of the round number.

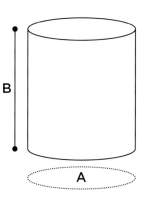

A   22.5"

B   12"

COLOR SHOCK HAT

by Lisa Seifert

FINISHED MEASUREMENTS

18″ circumference × 8.5″ height; worn with up to 3″ negative ease, to fit up to 21″ head circumference

YARN

Knit Picks Palette™ (fingering weight, 100% Peruvian Highland Wool; 231 yards/50g): MC Cream 23730, C1 Cyan 24583, C2 Majestic 24574, 1 ball each

NEEDLES

US 3 (3.25mm) 16″ circular needles and DPNs, or size to obtain gauge
US 1 (2.25mm) 16″ circular needles, or two sizes smaller than size used to obtain gauge

NOTIONS

Yarn Needle
Stitch Marker
3″ Pom-Pom Maker

GAUGE

28 sts and 32 rnds = 4″ in Stranded Stockinette Stitch in the round on larger needles, unblocked

For pattern support, contact happyindolevalley@gmail.com

Color Shock Hat

Notes:

Who doesn't love a little color? This vibrant beanie provides the perfect opportunity to add a bit of bold color to your wardrobe with its bright diamond zigzag bands. This hat is an ideal first colorwork project or a fun, quick knit for those with more experience.

The hat is knit in the round following the Alternate Cable Cast On and Setup Row, which are worked flat.

The chart is worked in the round; read each chart row from right to left as a RS row.

Alternate Cable Cast On

This cast on creates a stretchy edge that blends invisibly into your ribbing.

1. Start with a slip knot 6″ from end of yarn and place it on LH needle (counts as first CO st).

2. K into the slip knot; place the st you just created onto LH needle (do not twist now or throughout).

3. Insert RH needle from back to front between the 2 sts on LH needle; wrap yarn around needle and draw through, placing the P st you just created onto LH needle (do not twist now or throughout).

4. Insert RH needle from front to back between first 2 sts on LH needle; wrap yarn around needle and draw through, placing the K st you just created onto LH needle.

5. Insert RH needle from back to front between first 2 sts on LH needle; wrap yarn around needle and draw through, placing the P st you just created onto LH needle.

Rep Steps 4-5 until required number of sts have been CO.

DIRECTIONS

Brim

With MC and smaller needles, CO 126 sts using the Alternate Cable Cast On method.

Setup Row: Working flat, (K1 TBL, P1) to end of row; PM and join to work in the rnd, being careful not to twist sts.

Rnds 1-14: Work 1x1 Rib.

Body

Rnds 15-24: Switch to larger needles and work St st.

Rnds 25-48: Work Rnds 1-24 of Color Shock Chart, repeating chart sts 21 times per rnd.

Rnds 49-50: K all.

Crown

Rnd 51 (Setup Rnd): (K21, PM) five times, K21.

Rnd 52: (K2tog, K to 2 sts before M, SSK, SM) six times. 114 sts.

Rnds 53-54: K all.

Rnds 55-69: Rep Rnds 52-54 five times. 54 sts.

Rnd 70: Rep Rnd 52. 42 sts.

Rnd 71: K all.

Rnd 72: Rep Rnd 52. 30 sts.

Rnd 73: K all.

Rnd 74: Rep Rnd 52. 18 sts.

Rnd 75: K2tog to end of rnd. 9 sts.

Cut yarn leaving a 6″ tail and thread onto yarn needle. Sew through remaining sts, and pull snug to securely close top of hat.

Finishing

Neatly seam together gap from CO and Setup rows.

Weave in ends and gently wet block to finished measurements.

Pom-Pom

Using all three colors of yarn, make pom-pom and attach it securely to top of hat.

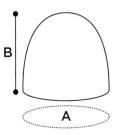

A 18″

B 8.5″

LEGEND

☐ Main Color (Cream)

▦ Contrasting Color 1 (Cyan)

■ Contrasting Color 2 (Majestic)

☐ Knit Stitch

Color Shock Chart

6	5	4	3	2	1	
▦	☐	☐	☐	▦	☐	24
▦	☐	☐	▦	☐	▦	23
▦	▦	☐	▦	▦	▦	22
▦	▦	■	▦	▦	▦	21
■	■	■	■	▦	▦	20
■	■	▦	■	■	▦	19
■	■	▦	■	■	■	18
■	▦	▦	▦	■	■	17
▦	▦	▦	▦	▦	■	16
▦	▦	▦	▦	▦	☐	15
☐	▦	▦	☐	▦	▦	14
▦	☐	▦	☐	▦	▦	13
▦	▦	☐	▦	▦	▦	12
▦	▦	☐	▦	▦	▦	11
▦	▦	☐	▦	▦	▦	10
▦	▦	■	▦	▦	▦	9
▦	▦	■	■	▦	▦	8
▦	■	■	■	■	▦	7
■	■	▦	■	▦	▦	6
▦	■	▦	▦	▦	■	5
▦	▦	▦	▦	▦	■	4
▦	▦	▦	▦	▦	☐	3
☐	▦	▦	▦	☐	☐	2
☐	▦	▦	☐	☐	☐	1

FLASH COWL & MITTS

by Kathy Lewinski

FINISHED MEASUREMENTS

Cowl 22″ circumference × 9.5″ height
Mitts 7 (7.5, 8)″ circumference × 8.5″ length

YARN

Knit Picks Palette™ (fingering weight,
100% Peruvian Highland Wool; 231
yards/50g): MC Asphalt Heather 24243,
2 balls; C1 White 23728, C2 Serrano
24553, C3 Canary 25531, 1 ball each

NEEDLES

Cowl US 2 (3mm) 16″ circular needles,
or size to obtain gauge

Mitts US 2 (3mm) DPNs or two 24″
circular needles for two circulars
technique or 32″ or longer circular
needles for Magic Loop technique,
or size to obtain gauge

NOTIONS

Yarn Needle
Stitch Marker
Contrasting Scrap Yarn

GAUGE

32 sts and 42 rnds = 4″ in Stranded
Stockinette Stitch in the round, blocked

For pattern support, contact jcraftyenough@gmail.com

Flash Cowl & Mitts

Notes:

Traditional Fair Isle looks modern and graphic when worked in dark gray and white with a flash of bright colors zig-zagging through the pattern.

Add or subtract repeats of the charts to make your cowl or mitts bigger in circumference. Each repeat is 0.5" wide. Both the cowl and the mitts are knit in the round working from the bottom to the top.

The charts are worked in the round; read each chart row from right to left as a RS row.

Jogless Colorwork for Knitting in the Round

Working in the round creates a jump or jog in the colorwork pattern at the beginning of a round whenever the color is changed. This can be minimized using the following technique.
Rnd 1: When starting new color on first st of rnd: K normally.
Rnd 2: Before knitting first st of rnd, bring st from rnd before up onto LH needle. Knit tog with first st of rnd.
Rep every time you change colors on first st of a rnd.

COWL DIRECTIONS

Bottom Edge

With MC on 16" circular needles, loosely CO 176 sts. Join to work in the rnd, being careful not to twist sts. PM for BOR.
Rnds 1-10: Work 2x2 Rib.

Body

With MC and C1, work Rnds 1-8 of Main Chart a total of eight times, repeating chart sts 44 times across rnd.
Using all the colors as charted, work Rnds 1-6 of Flash Chart. With MC and C1, work Rnds 7-8 and then Rnds 1-8 of Main Chart once more.
Break C1.

Top Edge

Work in MC.
Rnd 1: K all.
Rnds 2-11: Work 2x2 Rib.
BO loosely.

Finishing

Weave in ends, wash, and block.

MITTS DIRECTIONS

Bottom Edge

With MC, loosely CO 56 (60, 64) sts. Join to work in the rnd, being careful not to twist sts. PM for BOR.
Rnds 1-10: Work 2x2 Rib.

Wrist & Hand

With MC and C1, work Rnds 1-8 of Main Chart a total of six times, repeating chart sts 14 (15, 16) times across rnd.

Place Thumb

Left Hand: While working Rnd 1 of Main Chart, K1, K the next 13 (15, 15) sts with a piece of scrap yarn, slide those 13 (15, 15) sts back on to LH needle, K55 (59, 63).
Right Hand: While working Rnd 1 of Main Chart, K42 (44, 48), K the next 13 (15, 15) sts with a piece of scrap yarn, slide those 13 (15, 15) sts back on to LH needle, K14 (16, 16).

Finish Hand

Work Rnds 2-8 of Main Chart once more.
Using all the colors as charted, work Rnds 1-6 of Flash Chart. With MC and C1, work Rnds 7-8 and then Rnds 1-5 of Main Chart once more.
Break C1.

Top Edge

Work in MC.
Rnds 1-10: Work 2x2 Rib.
BO loosely.

Thumb

Work in MC.
Put the 13 (15, 15) sts above and the 13 (15, 15) sts below scrap yarn onto needles. Carefully remove scrap yarn. Arrange the 26 (30, 30) sts on needles to knit in the rnd, PM on right side between top and bottom sts to mark BOR.
Rnd 1: K13 (15, 15), PU and K 1 st from hand, K13 (15,15), PU and K 1 st from hand. 28 (32, 32) sts.
Rnds 2-11 Work 2x2 Rib.
BO loosely.

Finishing

Weave in ends, wash, and block.

LEGEND

⬛ Main Color (Asphalt Heather)

⬜ Contrasting Color 1 (White)

🟥 Contrasting Color 2 (Serrano)

🟨 Contrasting Color 3 (Canary)

⬜ Knit Stitch

Main Chart

4	3	2	1	
				8
				7
				6
				5
				4
				3
				2
				1

Flash Chart

4	3	2	1	
				6
				5
				4
				3
				2
				1

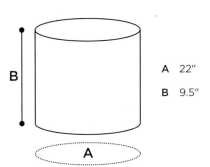

A 22"

B 9.5"

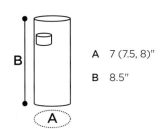

A 7 (7.5, 8)"

B 8.5"

NEUTRALITY HAT & COWL

by Natasha Sills

FINISHED MEASUREMENTS

Hat 18 (20, 22, 24)″ circumference × 9.25 (10.25, 11.25, 12.25)″ height
Cowl 28″ circumference × 12.5″ height

YARN

Knit Picks Palette™ (fingering weight, 100% Peruvian Highland Wool; 231 yards/50g): MC Cream 23730, 2 (2, 3, 3) balls; C1 Coriander Heather 25544, C2 Puma Heather 26059, C3 Grizzly Heather 25532, 2 balls each

NEEDLES

Hat US 1 (2.25mm) 16″ circular needles and DPNs, or size to obtain gauge
Cowl US 1 (2.25mm) 16″ or 24″ circular needles, or size to obtain gauge

NOTIONS

Yarn Needle
Stitch Markers, 1 unique
Pom-Pom Maker

GAUGE

32 sts and 48 rnds = 4″ in Stranded Stockinette Stitch in the round, blocked

For pattern support, contact natasha@grittyknits.com

Neutrality Hat & Cowl

Notes:

This hat and cowl are the perfect accessories for winter. The understated beauty and simple, classic designs are the perfect disguise of innocence before you ambush your friends in a good, old-fashioned snowball fight.

The wide selection of Palette yarn provides almost endless possibilities for color combinations, whether you are drawn to a subtle gradient or something much bolder.

The charts are worked in the round; read each chart row from right to left as a RS row.

HAT DIRECTIONS

Brim
Using C3, loosely CO 144 (160, 176, 192) sts.
PM for BOR and join in the rnd, being careful not to twist sts.
Rnds 1-18: (K1 TBL, P1) to end.

Body
Switch to MC.
Rnds 1-5: K all.
Rnds 6-18: Using MC and C3, work Snowflake Chart 1. Break C3.

Rnds 19-23: Using MC, K all.
Rnds 24-36: Using MC and C2, work Snowflake Chart 2. Break C2.

Rnds 37-41: Using MC, K all.
Rnds 42-54: Using MC and C1, work Snowflake Chart 1. Break C1.

Rnd 55: Using MC, K all.
Rep Rnd 55 until fabric measures 6.5 (7, 7.5, 8)" from CO edge.

Crown
Setup Rnd: *K18 (20, 22, 24) sts, PM; rep from * to end. (Be sure your BOR marker is unique.)
Rnd 1: K all.
Rnd 2: (SSK, K to M) to end.
Rep Rnds 1-2 until you have 8 sts remaining.

Break yarn and thread tail through remaining sts. Cinch together and secure with a knot.

Finishing
Weave in ends, wash, and block flat.

Pom-Pom
Follow the instructions included with your Knit Picks Pom-Pom maker, or use your chosen method.
To make a speckled pom as shown, use mostly MC and occasionally add in a few wraps of C1, C2, and C3. For example, 25 wraps of MC, 5 wraps of C1, 25 wraps of MC, 5 wraps of C2, 25 wraps of MC, 5 wraps of C3, etc. Repeat until very full—no one likes a droopy pom!

COWL DIRECTIONS

Ribbing
Using MC, loosely CO 224 sts.
PM for BOR and join in the rnd, being careful not to twist sts.
Rnds 1-18: (K1 TBL, P1) to end.

Body
Rnds 1-5: K all.
Rnds 6-18: Using MC and C1, work Snowflake Chart 1.
Rnds 19-23: Using MC, K all.
Rnds 24-36: Using MC and C1, work Snowflake Chart 2. Break C1.

Rnds 37-41: Using MC, K all.
Rnds 42-54: Using MC and C2, work Snowflake Chart 1.
Rnds 55-59: Using MC, K all.
Rnds 60-72: Using MC and C2, work Snowflake Chart 2. Break C2.

Rnds 73-77: Using MC, K all.
Rnds 78-90: Using MC and C3, work Snowflake Chart 1.
Rnds 91-95: Using MC, K all.
Rnds 96-108: Using MC and C3, work Snowflake Chart 2. Break C3.

Rnds 109-113: Using MC, K all.

Ribbing
Rnds 1-18: (K1 TBL, P1) to end.
Bind off.

Finishing
Weave in ends, wash, and block flat.

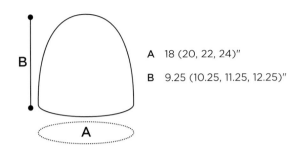

A 18 (20, 22, 24)"

B 9.25 (10.25, 11.25, 12.25)"

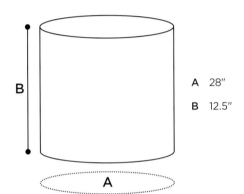

A 28"

B 12.5"

LEGEND

☐ Main Color

■ Contrasting Colors

☐ Knit Stitch

Snowflake Chart 1

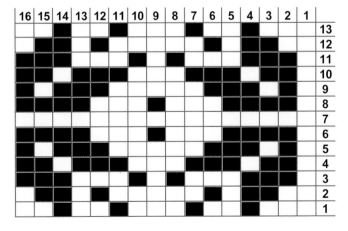

Snowflake Chart 2

CHURCHYARD RAILING HAT

by Becky Greene

FINISHED MEASUREMENTS
18 (20, 22, 24)" circumference × 9"
height; meant to be worn slouchy

YARN
Knit Picks Palette™ (fingering weight,
100% Peruvian Highland Wool; 231
yards/50g): MC Mist 23733, C1 Eggplant
24255, C2 Celestial 24582, C3 Cyan
24583, C4 Grass 24585, C5 Canary 25531,
C6 Orange 24554, C7 Serrano 24553,
1 ball each

NEEDLES
US 2 (2.75mm) DPNs and 16" circular
needles, or size to obtain gauge

NOTIONS
Yarn Needle
Stitch Markers

GAUGE
32 sts and 40 rnds = 4" in Stranded
Stockinette Stitch in the round,
gently blocked

For pattern support, contact greenethumb459@gmail.com

Churchyard Railing Hat

Notes:

The colorwork pattern on this hat lends itself to a myriad of colorful possibilities. Knit it in a cheerful rainbow of hues offset with white or black, use a monochromatic set of shades for a more sophisticated look, get scrappy with leftovers from your stash, or select jewel tones paired with black for a stained glass look. Whatever suits your tastes!

The pattern itself is surprisingly simple with its four-stitch repeat, ensuring a quick knit and a good choice for even an advanced beginning knitter.

The charts are worked in the round; read each chart row from right to left as a RS row.

DIRECTIONS

Brim

Loosely CO 108 (120, 132, 144) sts with MC on circular needle. PM and join to work in the rnd, being careful not to twist sts.

Rnds 1-10: Work 2x2 Rib.
Rnd 11: (K3, M1L) to end of rnd. 144 (160, 176, 192) sts.
Rnd 12: K all.

Body

Begin to work from Chart 1. Chart is worked 36 (40, 44, 48) times across rnd. Carry yarns loosely across back. Work Rnds 1-52 of Chart 1.

Crown

Switch to Chart 2. Chart is worked 9 (10, 11, 12) times across rnd. Cont to work color pattern, decreasing as indicated. Switch to DPNs as desired when circumference is too small to fit comfortably on circular needles.

After working Rnd 27, break yarn leaving a 6″ tail. Thread onto a yarn needle and run through remaining 9 (10, 11, 12) sts several times. Pull tightly to close up hole.

Finishing

Weave in loose ends, wash, and block gently.

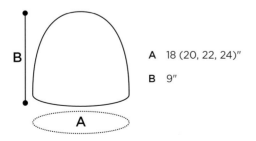

A   18 (20, 22, 24)″

B   9″

LEGEND

☐ Main Color (Mist)

■ Contrasting Color 1 (Eggplant)

■ Contrasting Color 2 (Celestial)

▨ Contrasting Color 3 (Cyan)

■ Contrasting Color 4 (Grass)

▨ Contrasting Color 5 (Canary)

▨ Contrasting Color 6 (Orange)

▨ Contrasting Color 7 (Serrano)

■ **No Stitch**
Placeholder—no stitch made

☐ **Knit Stitch**

◿ **K2tog**
Knit 2 stitches together as one stitch

◺ **SSK**
Slip, slip, knit slipped stitches together

△ **CDD**
Slip first and second stitches together
as if to K2tog; knit 1 stitch; pass 2
slipped stitches over the knit stitch

Body

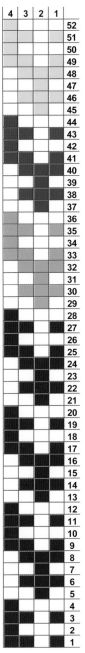

Decreases

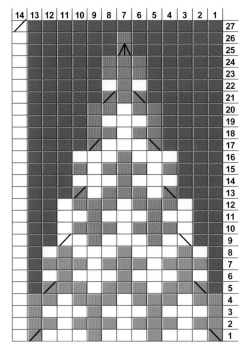

FOUR SEASONS
HAT & MITTS

by Lisa Seifert

FINISHED MEASUREMENTS

Hat 18.75" circumference × 8" height; worn with up to 3.25" negative ease, to fit up to 22" head circumference
Mitts 7.5" palm circumference × 7" length; worn with up to 1.5" negative ease, to fit up to 9" palm circumference

YARN

Knit Picks Palette™ (fingering weight, 100% Peruvian Highland Wool; 231 yards/50g): MC Clarity 25548, C1 Autumn Heather 24002, C2 Salsa Heather 24003, C3 Golden Heather 24005, 1 ball each

NEEDLES

Hat US 3 (3.25mm) 16" circular needles and DPNs, or size to obtain gauge
US 1 (2.25mm) 16" circular needles, or two sizes smaller than size used to obtain gauge

Mitts US 2 (2.75 mm) DPNs, or size to obtain gauge
US 0 (2mm) DPNs, or two sizes smaller than size used to obtain gauge

NOTIONS

Yarn Needle
Stitch Markers
3" Pom-Pom Maker
Scrap Yarn

GAUGE

Hat 27 sts and 30 rnds = 4" in Stranded Stockinette Stitch in the round, unblocked
Mitts 30 sts and 34 rnds = 4" in Stranded Stockinette Stitch in the round, unblocked

For pattern support, contact happyindolevalley@gmail.com

Four Seasons Hat & Mitts

Notes:

Four Seasons was designed to capture the beauty of leaves as they change color from season to season—from the pale shades of winter and spring to the bright colors of summer and autumn, the possibilities are endless!

Following the Alternate Cable Cast On and Setup Row, which are knit flat, the hat and mitts are knit in the round. The mitts are worked with smaller needles than the hat to accommodate the stitch pattern as well as for a better fit; they are designed "un-handed" to fit either your left or right hand.

The charts are worked in the round; read each chart row from right to left as a RS row.

Alternate Cable Cast On

This cast on creates a stretchy edge that blends invisibly into your ribbing.

1. Start with a slip knot 6″ from end of yarn and place it on LH needle (counts as first CO st).

2. K into the slip knot; place the st you just created onto LH needle (do not twist now or throughout).

3. Insert RH needle from back to front between the 2 sts on LH needle; wrap yarn around needle and draw through, placing the P st you just created onto LH needle (do not twist now or throughout).

4. Insert RH needle from front to back between first 2 sts on LH needle; wrap yarn around needle and draw through, placing the K st you just created onto LH needle.

5. Insert RH needle from back to front between first 2 sts on LH needle; wrap yarn around needle and draw through, placing the P st you just created onto LH needle.

Rep Steps 4-5 until required number of sts have been CO.

Latvian Braid

Rnd 1 (Setup): (K1 with C1, K1 with MC) to end of rnd.

Rnd 2: WYIF, P1 with C1, bring MC under C1 and P1 with MC, (bring C1 under MC and P1 with C1, bring MC under C1 and P1 with MC) to end of rnd. (Yarn strands will be twisted, but will untwist as you work next rnd.)

Rnd 3: Cont WYIF, P1 with C1, bring MC over C1 and P1 with MC, (bring C1 over MC and P1 with C1, bring MC over C1 and P1 with MC) to end of rnd. (Yarn strands should now be fully untwisted.)

Two Color Bind Off

K1 with C1, bring MC in front of C1 and K1, BO first st. Bring C1 in front of MC and K1, BO second st. Cont alternating between C1 and MC in this manner until all sts are BO.

HAT DIRECTIONS

Brim

With C1 and smaller needles, CO 126 sts using the Alternate Cable Cast On method.

Setup Row: Working flat, (K1 TBL, P1) to end of row; PM and join to work in the rnd, being careful not to twist sts.

Rnds 1-8: Work 1x1 Rib.

Rnds 9-11: Switch to larger needles, join MC, work Latvian Braid Rnds 1-3.

Colorwork & Crown

Rnds 12-42: Work Rnds 1-31 of Chart A, nine times per rnd.

Rnds 43-56: Work Rnds 1-14 of Chart B, nine times per rnd (note: to set up for dec at beginning of chart Rnd 12, BOR M is moved; work chart Rnd 11 until 1 st remains, Sl1, remove M, return Sl st to LH needle, PM). Break C2. 90 sts.

Rnds 57-59: Join C1 with MC, work Latvian Braid. Break MC.

Rnd 60: Working with C1, remove M, Sl2 WYIB, PM, (K7, CDD) to end. 72 sts.

Rnds 61-63: K all.

Rnd 64: Remove M, Sl1 WYIB, PM, (K5, CDD) to end. 54 sts.

Rnds 65-66: K all.

Rnd 67: Remove M, Sl1 WYIB, PM, (K3, CDD) to end. 36 sts.

Rnds 68-69: K all.

Rnd 70: Remove M, Sl1 WYIB, PM, (K1, CDD) to end. 18 sts.

Rnd 71: K2tog to end. 9 sts.

Cut yarn leaving 6″ tail and thread onto yarn needle. Sew through remaining sts, and pull snug to securely close top of hat.

Finishing

Neatly seam together gap from CO and Setup rows. Weave in ends, wash, and gently wet block to finished measurements.

Pom-Pom

Using all four colors of yarn, make pom-pom and attach it securely to top of hat.

MITTS DIRECTIONS

Cuff

With C1 and smaller needles, CO 56 sts using the Alternate Cable Cast On method.

Setup Row: Working flat, (K1 TBL, P1) to end of row; PM and join to work in the rnd, being careful not to twist sts.

Rnds 1-8: Work 1x1 Rib.

Rnds 9-11: Switch to larger needles, join MC, work Latvian Braid Rnds 1-3.

Hand & Thumb Gusset

Rnds 12-18: Work Rows 1-7 of Chart A, four times per rnd.

Rnd 19: With MC M1R, PM for gusset, work next rnd of Chart A. 1 gusset st inc; 57 sts.

Rnd 20: With MC M1R, K1, M1L, SM, work Chart A. 2 gusset sts inc; 59 sts.

Rnds 21-22: With MC K to M, SM, work Chart A.

Rnd 23: With MC M1R, K to M, M1L, SM, work Chart A. 2 gusset sts inc; 61 sts.

Rnds 24-25: K to M, SM, work Chart A.

Rnds 26-46: Rep Rnds 23-25; after completing Chart A begin Chart C. 75 sts total; 19 gusset sts.

Rnd 47: SM, transfer 19 thumb gusset sts to scrap yarn, remove gusset M, work Chart C. 56 sts.

Rnds 48-56: Work Chart C. Break C2.

Rnds 57-59: Join C1, work Latvian Braid.

BO with MC and C1 using Two Color Bind Off.

Thumb

Setup Rnd: Sl 19 thumb sts from scrap yarn to three larger DPNs (7, 7, 5 sts each). With Needle 3, join MC, firmly PU and K 3 sts, K1, PM and join to work in the rnd. 22 sts.

Rnd 1: K to 5 sts before M, SSK, K1, K2tog, SM. 20 sts.

Rnds 2-4: K all.

Rnds 5-7: Join C1, work Latvian Braid.

BO with MC and C1 using Two Color Bind Off.

Second Mitt

Make second mitt same as first.

Finishing

Neatly seam together gap from CO and Setup rows. Weave in ends, wash, and gently wet block to finished measurements.

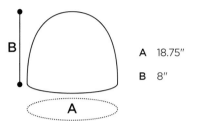

B

A   18.75"

B   8"

A

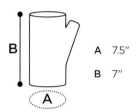

B

A   7.5"

B   7"

A

LEGEND

⬜ Main Color (Clarity)

◼ Contrasting Color 1 (Autumn Heather)

▦ Contrasting Color 2 (Salsa Heather)

▧ Contrasting Color 3 (Golden Heather)

◼ No Stitch
Placeholder—no stitch made

⬜ Knit Stitch

/Λ\ CDD
Slip first and second stitches together as if to K2tog;
knit 1 stitch; pass 2 slipped stitches over the knit stitch

Chart A

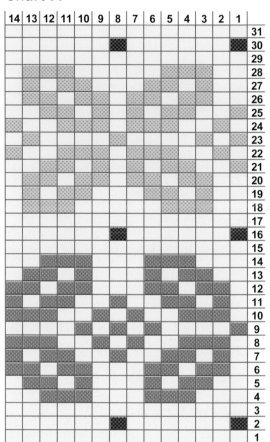

Chart B

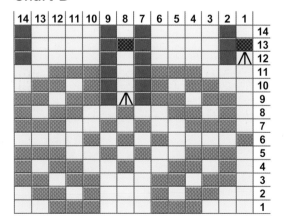

Chart C

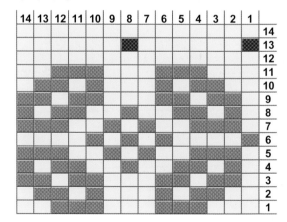

FAYRE SWEATER

by Claire Slade

FINISHED MEASUREMENTS

30.5 (33.75, 37.25, 40.5, 44, 47.5, 50.75, 54.25)" finished bust circumference; meant to be worn with no ease

YARN

Knit Picks Palette™ (fingering weight, 100% Peruvian Highland Wool; 231 yards/50g): MC Stellar 26053, 4 (4, 5, 6, 8, 9, 11, 12) balls; CC Clarity 25548, 1 (1, 1, 1, 2, 2, 2, 2) balls

NEEDLES

US 3 (3.25mm) 24" or longer circular needles and DPNs, or size to obtain gauge
US 2 (2.75mm) 24" or longer circular needles and DPNs, or one size smaller than size used to obtain gauge

NOTIONS

Yarn Needle
Stitch Markers
Scrap Yarn or Stitch Holders

GAUGE

26 sts and 30 rnds = 4" in Stockinette Stitch and Stranded Stockinette Stitch in the round on larger needles, blocked

For pattern support, contact verilyknits@gmail.com

Fayre Sweater

Notes:

Fayre's wide floral band appears to grow up from the sweater's lower hem, making for a visually interesting and unusual stranded colorwork sweater.

A short length fitted sweater with three-quarter length sleeves and a wide neckline, Fayre is knit in one piece, in the round from the top down, with raglan sleeves and waist shaping for a flattering and elegant fit.

The chart is worked in the round; read each row from right to left as a RS row.

DIRECTIONS

Yoke

Upper Edge

Using smaller needles and MC CO 126 (132, 134, 136, 138, 136, 138, 148) sts and join to work in the rnd, being careful not to twist sts.

Rnds 1-10: Work Garter Stitch.

Change to larger needles.

Raglan Shaping

Setup Rnd: *K53 (56, 57, 58, 59, 58, 59, 62), PM, K10 (10, 10, 10, 10, 10, 10, 12), PM; rep from * once more.

Sizes 37.25", 40.5", 44", 47.5", 50.75" & 54.25" Only

Rnd 1: (K1, KFB, K to 2 sts before M, KFB, K1, SM, KFB, K to 1 st before M, KFB, SM) two times. 8 sts inc.

Rep Rnd 1 - (-, 6, 10, 16, 19, 26, 26) more times. - (-, 190, 224, 274, 296, 354, 364) sts.

Sizes 30.5", 33.75" & 37.25" Only

Rnd 1: (K1, KFB, K to 2 sts before M, KFB, K1, SM, KFB, K to 1 st before M, KFB, SM) two times. 8 sts inc.

Rnd 2: (K to M, SM, KFB, K to 1 st before M, KFB, SM) two times. 4 sts inc.

Rep Rnds 1-2 5 (4, 1, -, -, -, -, -) more times. 198 (192, 214, 0, 0, 0, 0, 0) sts.

Resume All Sizes

Rnd 1: (K1, KFB, K to 2 sts before M, KFB, K1, SM, KFB, K to 1 st before M, KFB, SM) two times. 8 sts inc.

Rnd 2: K all.

Rep Rnds 1-2 12 (17, 17, 19, 18, 19, 17, 21) more times. 302 (336, 358, 384, 426, 456, 498, 540) sts.

Knit 4 (0, 0, 0, 0, 0, 0, 0) rnds.

Separate Sleeves

Next Rnd: K91 (102, 111, 120, 131, 138, 149, 160), remove M, CO 8 (8, 10, 12, 12, 16, 16, 16) sts, place next 60 (66, 68, 72, 82, 90, 100, 110) sts on scrap yarn or st holder for sleeve, remove M, K91 (102, 111, 120, 131, 138, 149, 160), remove M, CO 8 (8, 10, 12, 12, 16, 16, 16) sts, place next 60 (66, 68, 72, 82, 90, 100, 110) sts on separate scrap yarn or st holder for second sleeve, remove M. 198 (220, 242, 264, 286, 308, 330, 352) sts.

Body

Setup Section

Rnd 1: K95 (106, 116, 126, 137, 146, 157, 168), PM, K99 (110, 121, 132, 143, 154, 165, 176) PM for new BOR.

Rnds 2-10: K all.

Waist Shaping

Dec Rnd: (K1, K2tog, K to 3 sts before M, SSK, K1, SM) two times. 4 sts dec.

Knit seven rnds.

Rep these eight rnds four more times. 178 (200, 222, 244, 266, 288, 310, 332) sts.

Inc Rnd: (K1, M1L, K to 1 st before M, M1R, K1, SM) two times. 4 sts inc.

Knit four rnds.

Rep these five rnds four more times. On final rnd remove second M. 198 (220, 242, 264, 286, 308, 330, 352) sts.

Flower Section

Join C1 and work Rnds 1-32 of Fayre Chart.

Break MC and change to smaller needles.

Lower Edge

Rnds 1-11: Work Garter Stitch.

BO all sts.

Sleeves (make two the same)

With RS facing and using larger needles, return the held 60 (66, 68, 72, 82, 90, 100, 110) sts to needles and rejoin MC. CO 8 (8, 10, 12, 12, 16, 16, 16) sts and PM in the middle of these sts for BOR. 68 (74, 78, 84, 94, 106, 116, 126) sts.

Knit 8 (8, 6, 6, 6, 6, 5, 5) rnds.

Dec Rnd: K1, SSK, K to last 3 sts, K2tog, K1. 2 sts dec.

Rep these 9 (9, 7, 7, 7, 7, 6, 6) rnds 7 (8, 9, 9, 10, 10, 11, 11) more times. 52 (56, 58, 64, 72, 84, 92, 102) sts.

WE until sleeve measures 11" from underarm CO.

Break MC and change to smaller needles.

Cuff

Rnds 1-11: Using C1, work Garter Stitch.

BO all sts.

Finishing

Sew up both underarm seams.

Weave in all ends, wash, and block to diagram.

LEGEND

■ Main Color (Stellar Heather)

☐ Contrasting Color (Clarity)

☐ Knit Stitch

Fayre Chart

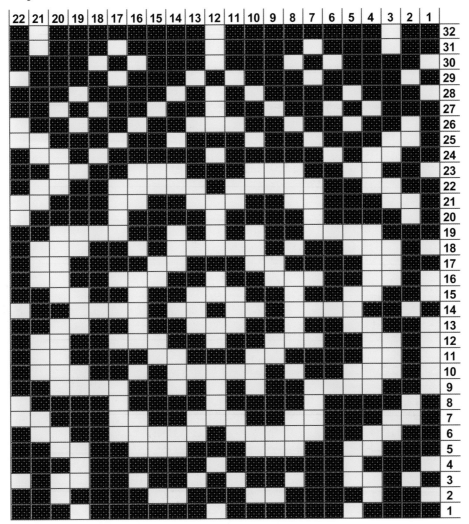

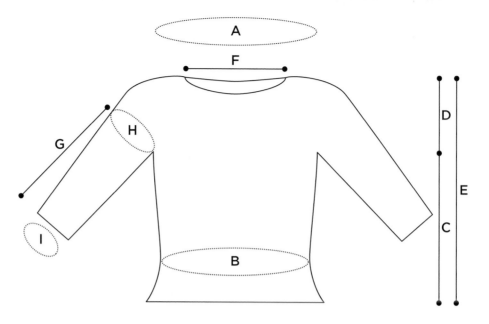

A   30.5 (33.75, 37.25, 40.5, 44, 47.5, 50.75, 54.25)"

B   27.5 (30.75, 34, 37.5, 41, 44.25, 47.75, 51)"

C   15"

D   7 (7.5, 7.75, 8.25, 8.75, 9.5, 10, 11.25)"

E   22 (22.5, 22.75, 23.25, 23.75, 24.5, 25, 26.25)"

F   9.75 (10.25, 10.25, 10.5, 10.5, 10.5, 10.5, 11.5)"

G   12.5"

H   10.5 (11.5, 12, 13, 14.5, 16.25, 17.75, 19.5)"

I   8 (8.5, 9, 9.75, 11, 13, 14.25, 15.75)"

MADRIGAL PULLOVER

by Claire Slade

FINISHED MEASUREMENTS

31.5 (35, 38.75, 41.75, 45.75, 50.25, 53.5)"
finished bust circumference; meant to
be worn with no ease

YARN

Knit Picks Palette™ (fingering weight,
100% Peruvian Highland Wool; 231
yards/50g): MC Finnley Heather 26043,
5 (5, 6, 7, 9, 10, 10) balls; CC Masala
24248, 1 (1, 1, 2, 2, 2, 3) balls

NEEDLES

US 3 (3.25mm) 24" or longer circular
needles and DPNs, or size to obtain gauge
US 2.5 (3mm) 24" or longer circular
needles and DPNs, or one size smaller
than size used to obtain gauge

NOTIONS

Yarn Needle
Stitch Markers
Scrap Yarn or Stitch Holder

GAUGE

26 sts and 30 rnds = 4" in Stockinette
Stitch and Stranded Stockinette Stitch
in the round on larger needles, blocked

For pattern support, contact verilyknits@gmail.com

Madrigal Pullover

Notes:

An ornate yoke pattern flows from the neckline like a magnificent baroque statement necklace. The gorgeous, intricate yoke and patterned edgings are all made with just two colors, keeping this project from being too intimidating, perfect for knitters ready to step up their colorwork skills.

Madrigal is knit in the round in one piece from the top down. The stranded colorwork of the yoke is the main focus of the sweater with subtler colorwork at both the hem and sleeves.

The charts are worked in the round; read each chart row from right to left as a RS row.

DIRECTIONS

Yoke

Upper Edge

Using CC and smaller needles, loosely CO 110 (120, 124, 124, 124, 132, 132) sts and join to work in the rnd, being careful not to twist sts.
Work 1x1 Rib in the rnd for 1".
Change to larger needles.

Setup

Size 38.75" Only
Next Rnd: (M1L, K20) six times, K4. 130 sts.

Size 41.75" Only
Next Rnd: (M1L, K8) 15 times, M1L, K4. 140 sts.

Size 53.5" Only
Next Rnd: (M1L, K11) twelve times. 144 sts.

Resume All Sizes
Knit 3 (3, 2, 3, 4, 5, 4) rnds.

Sizes 45.75", 50.25" & 53.5" Only
Next Rnd: (K4, M1R) to end. - (-, -, -, 155, 165, 180) sts.
Knit - (-, -, -, 2, 3, 4) rnds.

Main Yoke
Join MC and work Rnds 1-41 of Chart A once. 264 (288, 312, 336, 372, 396, 432) sts.
Work Rnds 1-6 of Chart B once, break CC. 308 (336, 364, 392, 434, 462, 504) sts.
Knit 4 (6, 10, 13, 15, 17, 20) rnds.

Separate for Sleeves
*K90 (100, 112, 122, 135, 145, 156), place next 64 (68, 70, 74, 82, 86, 96) sts onto scrap yarn or st holder for sleeve, CO 12 (14, 14, 14, 14, 18, 18) sts; rep from * once more. 204 (228, 252, 272, 298, 348) sts.

Body
WE in St st for 14 (14, 14, 15, 15, 15.5, 16)" from underarm.

A 31.5 (35, 38.75, 41.75, 45.75, 50.25, 53.5)"

B 7.25 (7.5, 8, 8.5, 9, 9.5, 10.25)"

C 16.5 (16.5, 16.5, 17.5, 17.5, 18, 18.5)"

D 19.5"

E 11.75 (12.5, 13, 13.5, 14.75, 16, 17.5)"

F 8.25 (9.25, 9.25, 10.25, 11, 11, 11)"

G 17 (18.5, 19, 19, 19, 20.5, 20.5)"

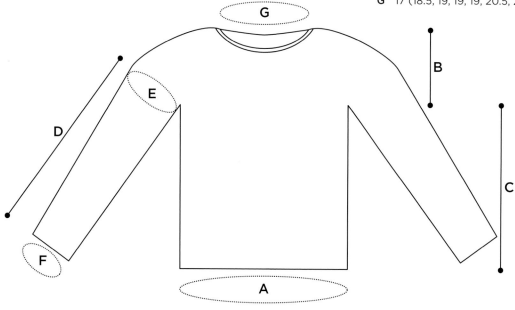

Lower Edge

Next Rnd: K decreasing 0 (0, 0, 2, 4, 2, 0) sts. - (-, -, 270, 294, 324, -) sts.
Join CC and work Rnds 1-10 of Chart C once, break MC.
Using CC, knit one rnd.
Change to smaller needles.
Work 1x1 Rib for 1".
BO all sts in pattern.

Sleeves (make two the same)

With RS facing return the held 64 (68, 70, 74, 82, 86, 96) sts to larger needles and rejoin MC.
CO 6 (7, 7, 7, 7, 9, 9) sts, PM for BOR, CO 6 (7, 7, 7, 7, 9, 9) sts. 76 (82, 84, 88, 96, 104, 114) sts.

Sleeve Decreases

Knit 10 (10, 9, 10, 9, 7, 5) rnds.
Dec Rnd: K1, SSK, K to last 3 sts, K2tog, K1. 2 sts dec.
Rep these 11 (11, 10, 11, 10, 8, 6) rnds 10 (10, 11, 10, 11, 15, 20) more times. 54 (60, 60, 66, 72, 72, 72) sts.
WE until work measures 17" from underarm CO, or 2.5" shorter than desired length.

Sleeve Edge

Join CC and work Rnds 1-10 of Chart C once, break MC.
Using CC, knit one rnd.
Change to smaller needles.
Work 1x1 Rib for 1".
BO all sts in pattern.

Finishing

Sew up both underarm seams.
Weave in all ends, wash, and block to diagram.

Chart A

LEGEND

- ☐ **Main Color (Finnley Heather)**
- ▨ **Contrasting Color (Masala)**
- ■ **No Stitch** — Placeholder—no stitch made
- ☐ **Knit Stitch**
- Ⓜ **M1L** — Make 1 left-leaning stitch

Chart B

Chart C

PIPER'S CREEK PULLOVER

by Allison Griffith

FINISHED MEASUREMENTS

33.25 (37.75, 41.5, 46, 50, 54.5, 58.25, 63.25, 67.25, 71)" finished bust circumference; meant to be worn with 4" positive ease

YARN

Knit Picks Palette™ (fingering weight, 100% Peruvian Highland Wool; 231 yards/50g): MC Mist 23733, 5 (5, 6, 6, 7, 7, 8, 8, 9, 9) balls; C1 Cosmopolitan 24568, C2 Shoal 26054, C3 Clarity 25548, C4 Wonderland Heather 26044, C5 Caribbean 25095, C6 Marina 25547, 1 ball each

NEEDLES

US 3 (3.25mm) 16", 24", and 32" circular needles and DPNs, or size to obtain gauge US 2 (2.75mm) 16" and 24" circular needles and DPNs, or one size smaller than size used to obtain gauge

NOTIONS

Yarn Needle
Stitch Marker
Scrap Yarn for Provisional CO
Scrap Yarn or Stitch Holder

GAUGE

25 sts and 34 rnds = 4" in Stockinette Stitch and Stranded Stockinette Stitch in the round on larger needles, blocked

For pattern support, contact knittingontheneedles@gmail.com

Piper's Creek Pullover

Notes:

This comfortable everyday pullover is a timeless sweater that celebrates color! The geometric design provides an excellent framework for all the colors of Palette that you love. A generous band of colorwork knitting around the shoulders makes this sweater fun to wear and interesting to knit, while the simple construction makes the project fly by. Suited for playing with contrasting colors or gradients of a favorite hue, this is a fun, modern sweater with roots in traditional Fair Isle knitting.

This sweater is worked from the top down in one piece, starting with a provisional cast on. The shoulders are shaped with short rows, followed by the colorwork yoke. The body is worked without further shaping, ending with a ribbed hem. The arms are knit from stitches set aside after working the yoke. Finally, the provisional cast on at the neck is removed and those live stitches are worked to create the collar.

The charts are worked in the round; read each chart row from right to left as a RS row.

DIRECTIONS

Yoke

With the larger 16" circular needles and MC, use scrap yarn and a Provisional Cast On to CO 80 (88, 104, 112, 120, 136, 144, 152, 168, 176) sts. PM for BOR and prepare to work in the rnd, being careful not to twist sts.

Rnd 1: K all.

Rnd 2: (K2, M1) to end. 120 (132, 156, 168, 180, 204, 216, 228, 252, 264) sts.

Rnd 3: K all.

Short Row Shoulder Shaping

Work short rows as follows, working wraps as you come to them.

Short Row 1 (RS): K26 (30, 35, 40, 43, 47, 52, 55, 59, 64), W&T.

Short Row 2 (WS): P to M, P26 (30, 35, 40, 43, 47, 52, 55, 59, 64), W&T.

Short Row 3: K to M.

Knit one rnd.

Short Row 4 (RS): K35 (40, 44, 48, 52, 56, 60, 64, 68, 73), W&T.

Short Row 5 (WS): P to M, P35 (40, 44, 48, 52, 56, 60, 64, 68, 73), W&T.

Short Row 6: K to M.

Knit one rnd.

Short Row 7 (RS): K42 (47, 51, 56, 59, 63, 68, 71, 75, 79), W&T.

Short Row 8 (WS): P to M, P42 (47, 51, 56, 59, 63, 68, 71, 75, 79), W&T.

Short Row 9: K to M.

Knit one rnd.

Work Piper's Creek Chart A (A, A, A, B, B, B, C, C, C). Join and break colors as necessary. Switch to longer larger circular needles when necessary. 300 (330, 390, 420, 450, 510, 540, 570, 630, 660) sts.

Cont in St st with MC until sweater measures 8 (8, 8.25, 8.25, 8.5, 9.5, 10, 10.5, 10.75, 11)" from front CO edge.

Split for Sleeves

Next Rnd: K45 (51, 57, 63, 69, 75, 81, 88, 94, 100) for Back Right, Sl 60 (63, 81, 84, 87, 105, 108, 109, 127, 130) sts onto st holder or scrap yarn for Right Sleeve, use Backward Loop Cast On to CO 14 (16, 16, 18, 18, 20, 20, 22, 22, 22) sts for Right Underarm, K90 (102, 114, 126, 138, 150, 162, 176, 188, 200) for Front, Sl 60 (63, 81, 84, 87, 105, 108, 109, 127, 130) sts to st holder or scrap yarn for Left Sleeve, use Backward Loop Cast On to CO 14 (16, 16, 18, 18, 20, 20, 22, 22, 22) sts for Left Underarm, K45 (51, 57, 63, 69, 75, 81, 88, 94, 100) for Back Left. 208 (236, 260, 288, 312, 340, 364, 396, 420, 444) sts.

Body

Knit all rnds until sweater measures 15 (15, 15.5, 15.5, 16, 16, 16.5, 16.5, 17, 17)" from underarm, or 2" shorter than desired length.

Switch to smaller 24" circular needles and work 1x1 Rib for 2". BO loosely in pattern.

Sleeves (make two the same)

Transfer 60 (63, 81, 84, 87, 105, 108, 109, 127, 130) sleeve sts from holder to larger 16" circular needles or larger DPNs. Beginning at center of underarm, PU and K 7 (8, 8, 9, 9, 10, 10, 11, 11, 11) sts, K60 (63, 81, 84, 87, 105, 108, 109, 127, 130) around sleeve, PU and K 7 (9, 9, 9, 10, 11, 10, 12, 12, 11) more sts from underarm, PM for BOR. 74 (80, 98, 102, 106, 126, 128, 132, 150, 152) sts.

Work in St st for 5 (5, 10, 10, 10, 5, 10, 20, 20, 20) rnds.

Decrease Rnds

Dec Rnd: K1, SSK, K to 3 sts before M, K2tog, K1, SM. 2 sts dec. Cont in St st, working a Dec Rnd every 10 (11, 7, 7, 7, 6, 6, 6, 5, 5) rnds until you have worked 14 (13, 20, 19, 19, 26, 24, 22, 29, 27) total Dec Rnds. Switch to larger DPNs when necessary. 46 (54, 58, 64, 68, 74, 80, 88, 92, 98) sts.

Cont in St st without decs, until sleeve measures 18 (18, 18.5, 18.5, 19, 19, 19.5, 19.5, 20, 20)" from underarm, or 2" shorter than desired length.

Switch to smaller DPNs and work 1x1 Rib for 2". BO loosely in pattern.

LEGEND

- ☐ Main Color (Mist)
- ▨ Contrasting Color 1 (Cosmopolitan)
- ■ Contrasting Color 2 (Shoal)
- ☐ Contrasting Color 3 (Clarity)
- ▨ Contrasting Color 4 (Wonderland Heather)
- ▨ Contrasting Color 5 (Caribbean)
- ▨ Contrasting Color 6 (Marina)
- ▨ No Stitch
  Placeholder—no stitch made
- ☐ Knit Stitch
- M M1L
  Make 1 left-leaning stitch

Piper's Creek Chart C

Piper's Creek Chart B

Piper's Creek Chart A

Collar

Remove Provisional Cast On and transfer the live sts to smaller 16" circular needles. 80 (88, 104, 112, 120, 136, 144, 152, 168, 176) sts.

Work 1x1 Rib for .75".
BO loosely in pattern.

Finishing

Weave in ends, being careful not to disrupt the stranded colorwork pattern.
Wash and block to diagram.

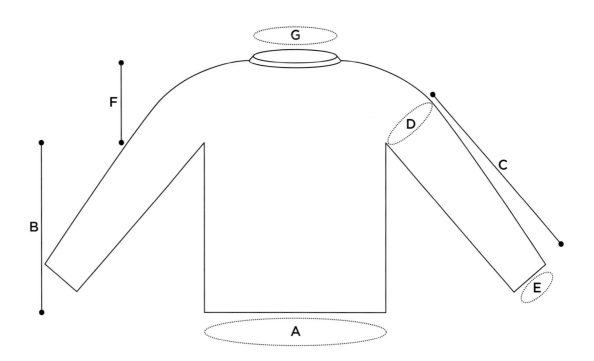

A   33.25 (37.75, 41.5, 46, 50, 54.5, 58.25, 63.25, 67.25, 71)"

B   17 (17, 17.5, 17.5, 18, 18, 18.5, 18.5, 19, 19)"

C   20 (20, 20.5, 20.5, 21, 21, 21.5, 21.5, 22, 22)"

D   11.75 (12.75, 15.75, 16.25, 17, 20, 20.5, 21.25, 24, 24.25)"

E   7.25 (8.75, 9.25, 10.25, 11, 11.75, 12.75, 14, 14.75, 15.5)"

F   8 (8, 8.25, 8.25, 8.5, 9.5, 10, 10.5, 10.75, 11)"

G   12.75 (14, 16.5, 18, 19.25, 21.75, 23, 24.25, 26.75, 28.25)"

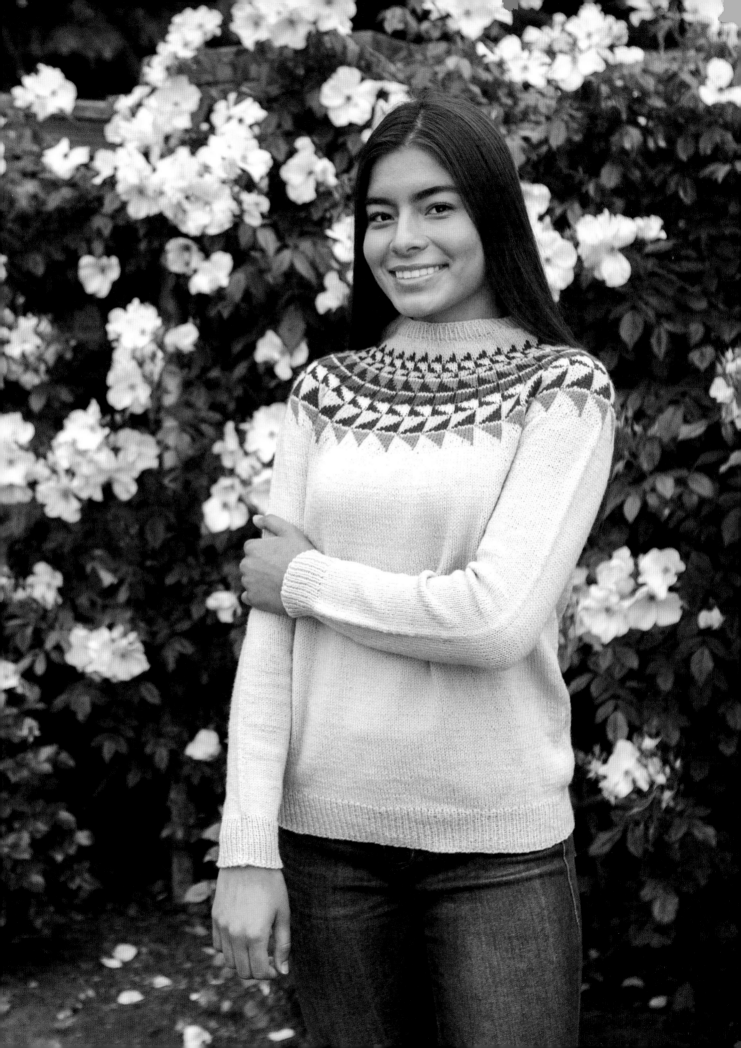

FLURRIES
SCARF & COWL

by Kendra Nitta

FINISHED MEASUREMENTS

Scarf 58″ length × 8.75″ width, excluding fringe
Cowl 22″ circumference × 8.75″ height

YARN

Knit Picks Palette™ (fingering weight, 100% Peruvian Highland Wool; 231 yards/50g): MC Mist 23733, C1 Bluebell 24578, 2 balls each for Scarf, 1 ball each for Cowl; C2 Semolina 24250, C3 White 23728, C4 Ash 23731, 1 ball each

NEEDLES

Scarf US 3 (3.25mm) 32″ or longer circular needles, or size to obtain gauge
Cowl US 3 (3.25mm) 16″ circular needles, or size to obtain gauge

NOTIONS

Yarn Needle
Stitch Markers
Crochet Hook

GAUGE

28 sts and 38 rnds = 4″ in Stranded Stockinette Stitch in the round, blocked

For pattern support, contact missknitta@gmail.com

Flurries Scarf & Cowl

Notes:

Flurries Scarf is worked in the round from long edge to long edge, then steeked open to turn it into a flat piece— a perfect introduction to steeking for knitters who may be timid about trying the technique. This project knits up surprisingly quickly, with just 63 rounds of colorwork and only a couple of ends to weave in. The pattern also contains an even quicker cowl version (no steeking needed!).

The fringe is created by dropping and cutting the steek stitches. This takes care of the loose ends, neatens the steeked edge without any sewing needed, and creates a fun design feature all at the same time.

A few rounds require the unused color to be carried for a large number of stitches. To keep the wrong side tidy and avoid snagging loose strands or "floats," be sure to secure floats every 3-4 stitches.

It is helpful to have at least two different types of stitch markers: one to mark the beginning and end of the steek, and one to mark the transitions between charts. You may also find it helpful to use a third type of marker for the pattern repeats in Bottom and Top Chart C.

The charts are worked in the round; read each chart row from right to left as a RS row.

Steek Stitches

This project includes a 30-stitch steek that will be unraveled at the end to make the fringe. Knit all steek stitches; on rounds with two colors, work steek stitches in alternating colors. All color changes should be made in the center of the steek. For example, when finishing a one-color round and preparing for a two-color round, work to the center of the steek and then join the second color. When changing colors in two-color knitting, work to the center of the steek with the colors from the round that is ending and join the new color at the center of the steek. (Joining or breaking yarn right before or after a charted stitch may result in the fringe being too short to knot at the end.)

SCARF DIRECTIONS

Bottom Edge

With C1, CO 432 sts.
Setup Row: K15, PM, (K3, P3) to last 15 sts; PM, K15, PM for BOR and join to work in the rnd. Note: The 30 sts between these Ms are steek sts that are always knit, and are not included in charts or in directions, unless otherwise noted. See Notes for how to work steek sts.

(K3, P3) for two more rnds.
(P3, K3) for three rnds.
(K3, P3) for three rnds.

Inc Rnd: K41, (M1R, K80) four times, M1R, K41. 407 sts, plus 30 steek sts.
Work Rnds 1-6 of Bottom Border Chart. The last rep of each rnd ends on the seventh st.

Body

Bottom Charts

Setup Rnd: Work Rnd 1 from Bottom Chart A, working pattern rep ten times, PM; work Rnd 1 from Bottom Chart B, break MC yarn and PM; work Rnd 1 from Bottom Chart C, working chart twelve times (weaving in MC end as you go), PM; join MC and work Rnd 1 from Bottom Chart D, PM; work Rnd 1 from Bottom Chart A, working pattern rep twelve times. It may be helpful to PMs between pattern reps for Chart C.

Cont working Bottom Charts in this order through Rnd 25.

Top Charts

Setup Rnd: Work Rnd 1 from Top Chart A, working pattern rep twelve times, PM; work Rnd 1 from Top Chart B, PM; work Rnd 1 from Top Chart C, working chart twelve times, PM; work Rnd 1 from Top Chart D, PM; work Rnd 1 from Top Chart A, working pattern rep ten times, removing Ms as needed.

Cont working Top Charts in this order through Rnd 25. Work Rnd 26, breaking MC yarn after Top Chart B, weaving in MC end as you work Top Chart C, then joining MC again for Top Charts D and A as before.

Top Edge

Work Rnds 1-6 of Top Border Chart. The last rep of each rnd ends on the seventh st.

Dec Rnd: With C1, K41, (K2tog, K79) four times, K2tog, K40. 402 sts, plus 30 steek sts.

(K3, P3) for three rnds.
(P3, K3) for three rnds.
(K3, P3) for three rnds.

K15 steek sts, BO 402 sts in pattern. Break yarn and pull through loop of last BO st. There will be 30 live steek sts still on the needle.

Finishing

Steek and Fringe

Drop 30 steek sts off needles and unravel all rows. Cut loose strands down the center.
Divide sts evenly into bundles of 6-8 strands each. With crochet hook, knot each bundle of strands, tidying tension on edge sts before knotting.

Weave in any remaining ends. Wash and block to measurements. Cut fringe to 3″ or desired length.

COWL DIRECTIONS

Bottom Edge

With C1, CO 150 sts. PM and join to work in the rnd, being careful not to twist sts.

(K3, P3) for three rnds.
(P3, K3) for three rnds.
(K3, P3) for three rnds.

Inc Rnd: (K37, M1R) four times, K2. 154 sts.

Work Rnds 1-6 of Bottom Border Chart, ending last rep on the second st.

Body

Bottom Charts

Setup Rnd: Work Rnd 1 from Bottom Chart D, PM; work Rnd 1 from Bottom Chart A, working pattern rep five times, PM; work Rnd 1 from Bottom Chart B, break MC yarn and PM; work Rnd 1 from Bottom Chart C, working chart five times (weaving in MC end as you go), PM. It may be helpful to PM between pattern reps for Chart C.

Join MC and cont working Bottom Charts in this order through Rnd 25, weaving in ends as you go.

Top Charts

Setup Rnd: Work Rnd 1 from Top Chart C (do not rep); work Rnd 1 from Top Chart D; work Rnd 1 from Top Chart A, working pattern rep five times, PM; work Rnd 1 from Top Chart B; work Rnd 1 from Top Chart C, working chart four times, removing Ms as needed.

Cont working Top Charts in this order through Rnd 25, break MC yarn.

Work Rnd 26, joining MC for Top Charts D, A, and B as before, then breaking yarn after Chart B.

Top Edge

Work Rnds 1-6 of Top Border Chart, ending last rep on the second st.

Dec Rnd: With C1, (K36, K2tog) four times, K2. 150 sts.

(K3, P3) for three rnds.
(P3, K3) for three rnds.
(K3, P3) for three rnds.
BO in pattern.

Finishing

Weave in ends. Wash and block to measurements.

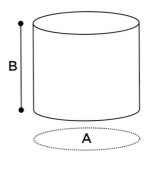

A 58"
B 8.75"

A 22"
B 8.75"

Bottom Border Chart

	8	7	6	5	4	3	2	1	
									6
									5
									4
									3
									2
									1

LEGEND

⬜ Main Color (Mist)

⬛ Contrasting Color 1 (Bluebell)

⬜ Contrasting Color 2 (Semolina)

⬜ Contrasting Color 3 (White)

⬛ Contrasting Color 4 (Ash)

⬜ Knit Stitch

⬜ Pattern Repeat

Bottom Chart A

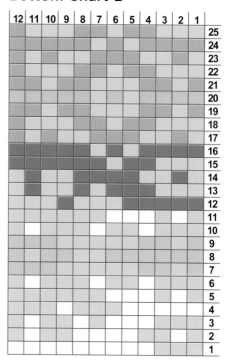

Scarf: Rep ten times at beginning of rnd, twelve times at end of rnd.
Cowl: Rep five times.

Bottom Chart B

Bottom Chart C

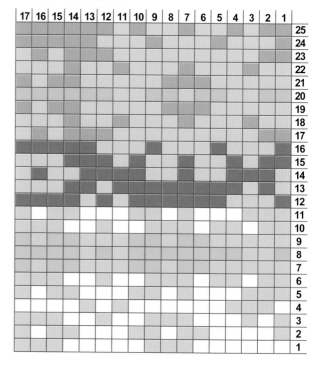

Bottom Chart D

Top Chart A

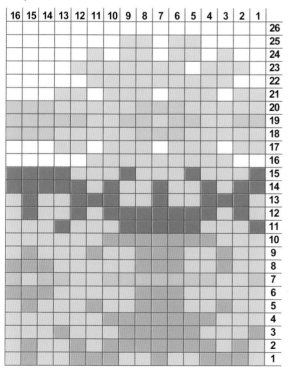

13	12	11	10	9	8	7	6	5	4	3	2	1	
													26
													25

Scarf: Rep ten times at beginning of rnd, twelve times at end of rnd.

Cowl: Rep five times.

Top Chart B

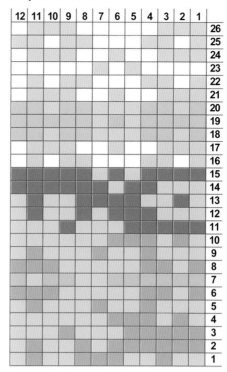

12	11	10	9	8	7	6	5	4	3	2	1	

Top Chart C

16	15	14	13	12	11	10	9	8	7	6	5	4	3	2	1	

Top Chart D

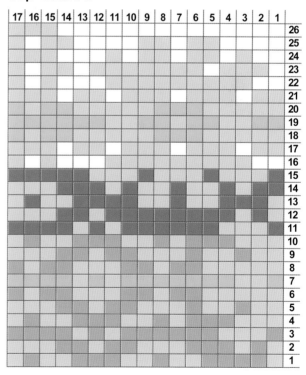

17	16	15	14	13	12	11	10	9	8	7	6	5	4	3	2	1	

Top Border Chart

8	7	6	5	4	3	2	1	
								6
								5
								4
								3
								2
								1

ABBEY ROAD SWEATER

by Beverley Dott

FINISHED MEASUREMENTS

38.25 (42.25, 46.25, 50.25, 54.25, 58.25, 62.25, 66.25, 70.25)″ finished bust circumference; meant to be worn with 10″ positive ease

YARN

Knit Picks Palette™ (fingering weight, 100% Peruvian Highland Wool; 231 yards/50g): MC Clarity 25548, 2 (2, 3, 4, 5, 6, 7, 7, 8) balls; C1 Mulberry 24571, 1 (1, 2, 2, 3, 3, 4, 4, 4) balls; C2 Indigo Heather 26051, 2 (2, 3, 3, 4, 4, 4, 5, 5) balls; C3 Hyacinth 23721, 1 (1, 2, 2, 3, 3, 3, 4, 4) balls; C4 Midnight Heather 25540, 1 (1, 2, 3, 4, 4, 5, 5, 6) balls; C5 Lantana 24572, 1 (1, 1, 2, 2, 2, 2, 2, 3) balls; C6 Caribbean 25095, 1 (1, 1, 1, 1, 1, 1, 1, 2) balls; C7 Calypso Heather 24009, 1 (1, 1, 2, 2, 2, 3, 4, 5) balls; C8 Marine Heather 24010, 1 (1, 1, 1, 1, 1, 1, 1, 2) balls; C9 Pennyroyal 25090, 1 ball (additional yarn may be required for the thumbhole option)

NEEDLES

US 3 (3.25mm) 32″ or longer circular needles (depending on size knit) and DPNs or long circular needles for Magic Loop technique (for sleeves), or size to obtain gauge

US 2 (2.75mm) 32″ or longer circular needles (depending on size knit) and DPNs or long circular needles for Magic Loop technique (for sleeves), or one size smaller than size used to obtain gauge

US 3 (3.25mm) extra needle for 3-Needle Bind Off, or size to obtain gauge

NOTIONS

Yarn Needle
8 Stitch Markers
Stitch Holders or Scrap Yarn

GAUGE

32 sts and 35 rnds = 4″ in Stranded Stockinette Stitch in the round on larger needles, blocked

For pattern support, contact faircityknits@outlook.com

Abbey Road

Notes:

Abbey Road is a cozy sweater where the colors of the motifs reflect the color of Scottish wildflowers in the summertime.

A roomy, long sleeve, high-hip length, Fair Isle sweater, Abbey Road is designed to be worn with 10" of positive ease. It has an allover pattern that uses two different motifs throughout the body and sleeves. The body is worked in the round from the bottom up; the neck and armholes are steeked and shoulders are joined with a 3-Needle Bind Off. Stitches are picked up around the steeked armhole edge and sleeves are worked from the top down to the cuffs, which are finished in corrugated rib. Stitches are picked up around the neck and a corrugated rib neckband finishes off the body.

The colorwork patterns are written and charted. Charts are worked in the round; read each chart row from right to left as a RS row. In the written versions of the color patterns, K- C- = K- using C- yarn (e.g. K2 C1 means K2 sts in C1 yarn).

Abbey Road 1 (in the round over a multiple of 4 sts)
Rnds 1-2: K1 MC, P2 C2, K1 MC.
Rnds 3-4: K1 MC, P2 C1, K1 MC.
Rnds 5-6: K1 MC, P2 C5, K1 MC.
Rnds 7-8: K1 MC, P2 C3, K1 MC.
Rnds 9-10: K1 MC, P2 C9, K1 MC.
Rnds 11-12: K1 MC, P2 C6, K1 MC.
Rnds 13-14: K1 MC, P2 C7, K1 MC.
Rnds 15-16: K1 MC, P2 C8, K1 MC.
Rnds 17-18: K1 MC, P2 C4, K1 MC.

Abbey Road 2 (in the round over a multiple of 30 sts)
Rnd 1: Using MC, K all.
Rnd 2: K2 MC, K2 C1, K2 MC, K1 C1, K1 MC, K1 C1, K2 MC, K7 C1, K2 MC, K1 C1, K1 MC, K1 C1, K2 MC, K2 C1, K2 MC, K1 C1.
Rnd 3: K1 MC, K2 C1, K2 MC, K1 C1, K1 MC, K1 C1, K2 MC, K4 C1, K1 MC, K4 C1, K2 MC, K1 C1, K1 MC, K1 C1, K2 MC, K2 C1, K1 MC, K1 C1.
Rnd 4: K1 MC, K1 C2, K2 MC, K1 C2, K1 MC, K1 C2, K2 MC, K4 C2, K1 MC, K1 C2, K1 MC, K4 C2, (K2 MC, K1 C2, K1 MC, K1 C2) two times.
Rnd 5: K3 MC, K1 C2, K1 MC, K1 C2, K2 MC, K4 C2, (K1 MC, K1 C2) two times, K1 MC, K4 C2, K2 MC, K1 C2, K1 MC, K1 C2, K3 MC, K1 C2.
Rnd 6: K2 C3, K1 C2, K1 C3, K1 C2, K2 C3, K4 C2, K3 C3, K1 C2, K3 C3, K4 C2, K2 C3, K1 C2, K1 C3, K1 C2, K2 C3, K1 C2.
Rnd 7: (K1 C3, K1 C4) two times, K2 C3, K4 C4, K1 C3, K1 C4, K1 C3, K3 C4, K1 C3, K1 C4, K1 C3, K4 C4, K2 C3, (K1 C4, K1 C3) two times, K1 C4.
Rnd 8: K2 C3, K1 C4, K2 C3, K4 C4, K3 C3, K2 C4, K1 C3, K2 C4, K3 C3, K4 C4, (K2 C3, K1 C4) two times.
Rnd 9: K1 C5, K1 C4, K2 C5, K4 C4, K1 C5, K1 C4, K1 C5, K2 C4, K3 C5, K2 C4, K1 C5, K1 C4, K1 C5, K4 C4, K2 C5, K1 C4, K1 C5, K1 C4.
Rnd 10: K3 C5, K4 C6, (K1 C5, K1 C6, K1 C5, K3 C6) two times, K1 C5, K1 C6, K1 C5, K4 C6, K3 C5, K1 C6.
Rnd 11: Rep Rnd 9.

Rnd 12: Rep Rnd 8.
Rnd 13: Rep Rnd 7.
Rnd 14: Rep Rnd 6.
Rnd 15: Rep Rnd 5.
Rnd 16: Rep Rnd 4.
Rnd 17: Rep Rnd 3.
Rnd 18: Rep Rnd 2.
Rnd 19: Using MC, K all.

Abbey Road 3 (in the round over a multiple of 12 sts)
Rnd 1: Using C7, K all.
Rnd 2: K1 C2, K3 C7, K1 C2, K2 C7, K3 C2, K2 C7.
Rnd 3: (K1 C8, K1 C2) two times, K2 C8, (K2 C2, K1 C8) two times.
Rnd 4: K2 C8, K1 C9, K3 C8, (K1 C9, K1 C8) three times.
Rnd 5: Rep Rnd 3.
Rnd 6: Rep Rnd 2.
Rnd 7: Using C7, K all.

Abbey Road 4 (in the round over a multiple of 4 sts)
Rnd 1: K1 MC, P2 C2, K1 MC.
Rnd 2: K1 MC, P2 C1, K1 MC.
Rnd 3: K1 MC, P2 C5, K1 MC.
Rnd 4: K1 MC, P2 C3, K1 MC.
Rnd 5: K1 MC, P2 C9, K1 MC.
Rnd 6: K1 MC, P2 C6, K1 MC.
Rnd 7: K1 MC, P2 C7, K1 MC.
Rnd 8: K1 MC, P2 C8, K1 MC.
Rnd 9: K1 MC, P2 C4, K1 MC.

DIRECTIONS

Body
Hem
Using MC and larger needles, *CO 160 (176, 192, 208, 224, 240, 256, 272, 288) sts, PM; rep from * once more. 320 (352, 384, 416, 448, 480, 512, 544, 576) sts. Join to work in the rnd, being careful not to twist sts. Ms separate front and back, and will be where armhole steeks are CO.

Rnds 1-18: Work Abbey Road 1 pattern from written or chart, creating corrugated rib.
Rnd 19: Using MC, (K1, M1, K to M, SM) two times. 161 (177, 193, 209, 225, 241, 257, 273, 289) sts each for front and back; 322 (354, 386, 418, 450, 482, 514, 546, 578) sts total.

Main Body
Next Rnd: *Working from Rnd 1 of Abbey Road 2 pattern and starting on St 25 (17, 9, 1, 23, 15, 7, 29, 21), work to M, SM; rep from * once more.
Work Rnds 2-19 of Abbey Road 2 pattern as established.

Next Rnd: *Working from Rnd 1 of Abbey Road 3 pattern and starting on St 7 (11, 3, 7, 11, 3, 7, 11, 3), work to M, SM; rep from * once more.
Work Rnds 2-7 of Abbey Road 3 pattern as established.

At this point you may wish to use optional Ms to mark center sts to ensure that motifs line up throughout. Center st should be St 15 of Abbey Road 2 or St 3 of Abbey Road 3.
Rep the last 26 rnds until work measures 11 (11, 10.75, 10.5, 10.25, 10, 9.5, 9.5, 9)″ from CO edge.

Armhole Steeks
Cont to work patterns as established and set up armhole steeks as follows.
Setup Rnd: *Work to M, SM, CO 7 sts using Backward Loop Cast On; rep from * once more. 161 (177, 193, 209, 225, 241, 257, 273, 289) sts each for front and back, 7 steek sts at each side separating front from back; 336 (368, 400, 432, 464, 496, 528, 560, 592) sts total.
Next Rnd: *Work to M, SM, (K1 CC in use, K1 MC) three times, K1 CC in use; rep from * once more.
Cont to work in pattern until armhole steeks measure 6.5 (6.75, 7.25, 7.25, 7.75, 8, 8, 8.5, 9)″, with steek sts being worked in alternate colors as established.

Neck Shaping
Cont to work patterns as established and set up neckline steek, then work neck shaping as follows.
Setup Rnd: K58 (64, 69, 75, 81, 86, 92, 97, 103), K2tog, K1, Sl the following 39 (43, 49, 53, 57, 63, 67, 73, 77) center front sts onto st holder or scrap yarn, PM, CO 7 sts using Backward Loop Cast On for neckline steek, PM, K1, SSK, K58 (64, 69, 75, 81, 86, 92, 97, 103) sts to next M, work steek sts, work to end in pattern as established.

Next Rnd: K to first M, SM, (K1 CC in use, K1 MC) three times, K1 CC in use, SM, work to end in pattern.
Next Rnd: K to 3 sts before first M, K2tog, K1, SM, (K1 CC in use, K1 MC) three times, K1 CC in use, SM, K1, SSK, work to end in pattern. 2 sts dec, 1 on each side of neckline steek.
Rep the last two rnds 5 (6, 6, 7, 8, 8, 10, 10, 10) more times. 10 (12, 12, 14, 16, 16, 20, 20, 20) front sts dec.
WE 4 (4, 4, 6, 4, 6, 6, 6) more rnds without shaping.

Next Rnd: K54 (59, 64, 69, 74, 79, 83, 88, 94), SM, BO steek sts, SM, K54 (59, 64, 69, 74, 79, 83, 88, 94), SM, BO steek sts, SM, K54 (59, 64, 69, 74, 79, 83, 88, 94), SM, Sl next 53 (59, 65, 71, 77, 83, 91, 97, 101) back neck sts onto st holder or scrap yarn, work to M in pattern, SM, BO steek sts.

Join Shoulders
Turn Body section inside out, work 3-Needle Bind Off on larger needles to join each shoulder.

Steeks
Turn work inside out. Reinforce steeks using your preferred method. Using sharp scissors, cut up through the center st (St 4) of all three steeks. Fold back and join to main body with slip stitch, or finish as you like.

Sleeves (make two the same)
Sleeves are worked in the rnd from the top down, with dec sts at regular intervals, and corrugated rib at the cuff, with an option for working a longer sleeve with a thumb hole.

Using larger needles and C7, beginning at underarm, PU and K 109 (113, 119, 127, 139, 155, 167, 179, 179) sts around armhole opening, through the pattern sts next to the steek sts.

Sleeve Shaping
Decs and patterning are worked at the same time—read through entire section before beginning.
Work ten rnds without shaping first, as follows, then work the first Dec Rnd on the eleventh rnd.
Rnd 1: Working from Rnd 1 of Abbey Road 3 pattern and starting on St 9 (7, 4, 12, 6, 10, 4, 10, 10), work to end, PM for BOR.
Next 6 Rnds: Work Rnds 2-7 of Abbey Road 3 pattern.
Next 19 Rnds: Starting on St 21 (19, 16, 12, 6, 28, 22, 16, 16) work Rnds 1-19 of Abbey Road 2.
You may wish to use a M to mark center st, to ensure that motifs line up throughout; center st should be St 15 of Abbey Road 2 or St 3 of Abbey Road 3.

AT THE SAME TIME as repeating Abbey Road 3 then 2, work decs as follows.
Dec Rnd: K1, K2tog, work to 3 sts before end of rnd, SSK, K1. 2 sts dec.
Work Dec Rnd every two rnds a total of 6 (0, 6, 12, 18, 34, 46, 53, 53) times, then every four rnds a total of 20 (24, 21, 19, 17, 9, 3, 0, 0) times. 57 (65, 65, 65, 69, 69, 69, 73, 73) sts.
Cont working in patterns as established until work measures 12 (12.5, 12.5, 13, 13, 13.5, 13.5, 14, 14)″ from PU rnd.
If making optional thumbhole, work 5″ longer, in pattern as established.

Next Rnd: Using MC, K27 (32, 32, 34, 34, 34, 34, 36, 36), K2tog, K to end. 56 (64, 64, 68, 68, 68, 72, 72) sts.

Optional Thumbhole
Left Sleeve
BO Rnd: Using MC, K8 (10, 10, 10, 11, 11, 11, 12, 12), BO 12 sts, K36 (42, 42, 42, 45, 45, 45, 48, 48).
CO Rnd: Using MC, K8 (10, 10, 10, 11, 11, 11, 12, 12), CO 12 sts using Backward Loop Cast On, K36 (42, 42, 42, 45, 45, 45, 48, 48).

Right Sleeve
BO Rnd: Using MC, K36 (42, 42, 42, 45, 45, 45, 48, 48), BO 12 sts, K8 (10, 10, 10, 11, 11, 11, 12, 12).
CO Rnd: Using MC, K36 (42, 42, 42, 45, 45, 45, 48, 48), CO 12 sts using Backward Loop Cast On, K8 (10, 10, 10, 11, 11, 11, 12, 12) sts.

Cuff
Cuff Rnds 1-18: Using smaller needles, work Abbey Road 1 pattern.
BO using MC.

Neckband

Using smaller circular needles and MC, with RS of work facing, beginning at back right shoulder PU and K 16 (19, 19, 22, 23, 25, 29, 29, 31) sts down right side of neck, transfer 39 (43, 49, 53, 57, 63, 67, 73, 77) sts from front neck holder onto needle, PU and K 16 (19, 19, 22, 23, 25, 29, 29, 31) sts up left side of neck, transfer 53 (59, 65, 71, 77, 83, 91, 97, 101) sts from back neck holder onto needle, PM. 124 (140, 152, 168, 180, 196, 216, 228, 240) sts.

Rnds 1-9: Work Abbey Road 4 pattern.

BO using MC.

Finishing

Weave in ends.

Wash and block sweater to schematic measurements.

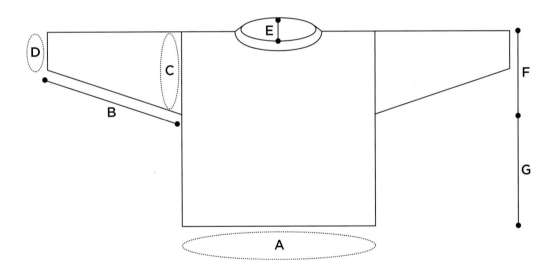

A   40.25 (44.25, 48.25, 52.25, 56.25, 60.25, 64.25, 68.25, 72.25)"

B   14 (14.5, 14.5, 15, 15, 15.5, 15.5, 16, 16)"

C   13.75 (14.25, 15, 16, 17.5, 19.5, 21, 22.5, 22.5)"

D   7 (8, 8, 8, 8.5, 8.5, 8.5, 9, 9)"

E   2 (2.25, 2.25, 2.75, 2.75, 3, 3.5, 3.5, 3.5)"

F   8.5 (9, 9.5, 10, 10.5, 11, 11.5, 12, 12.5)"

G   11 (11, 10.75, 10.5, 10.25, 10, 9.5, 9.5, 9)"

LEGEND

- ☐ Main Color (Clarity)
- ■ Contrasting Color 1 (Mulberry)
- ■ Contrasting Color 2 (Indigo Heather)
- ■ Contrasting Color 3 (Hyacinth)
- ■ Contrasting Color 4 (Midnight Heather)
- ■ Contrasting Color 5 (Lantana)
- ■ Contrasting Color 6 (Caribbean)
- ▦ Contrasting Color 7 (Calypso Heather)
- ■ Contrasting Color 8 (Marine Heather)
- ☐ Contrasting Color 9 (Pennyroyal)
- ☐ Knit Stitch
- ⦿ Purl Stitch

Abbey Road 1

4	3	2	1	
	●	●		18
	●	●		17
	●	●		16
	●	●		15
	●	●		14
	●	●		13
	●	●		12
	●	●		11
	●	●		10
	●	●		9
	●	●		8
	●	●		7
	●	●		6
	●	●		5
	●	●		4
	●	●		3
	●	●		2
	●	●		1

Abbey Road 2

30	29	28	27	26	25	24	23	22	21	20	19	18	17	16	15	14	13	12	11	10	9	8	7	6	5	4	3	2	1	
																														19
																														18
																														17
																														16
																														15
																														14
																														13
																														12
																														11
																														10
																														9
																														8
																														7
																														6
																														5
																														4
																														3
																														2
																														1

Abbey Road 3

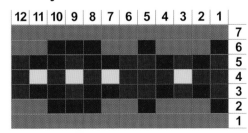

12	11	10	9	8	7	6	5	4	3	2	1	
												7
												6
												5
												4
												3
												2
												1

Abbey Road 4

4	3	2	1	
	●	●		9
	●	●		8
	●	●		7
	●	●		6
	●	●		5
	●	●		4
	●	●		3
	●	●		2
	●	●		1

Glossary
Common Stitches & Techniques

Slipped Stitches (Sl)
Always slip stitches purl-wise with yarn held to the wrong side of work, unless noted otherwise in the pattern.

Make 1 Left-Leaning Stitch (M1L)
Inserting LH needle from front to back, PU the horizontal strand between the st just worked and the next st, and K TBL.

Make 1 Right-Leaning Stitch (M1R)
Inserting LH needle from back to front, PU the horizontal strand between the st just worked and the next st, and K TFL.

Slip, Slip, Knit (SSK)
(Sl1 K-wise) twice; insert LH needle into front of these 2 sts and knit them together.

Centered Double Decrease (CDD)
Slip first and second sts together as if to work K2tog; K1; pass 2 slipped sts over the knit st.

Stockinette Stitch (St st, flat over any number of sts)
Row 1 (RS): Knit all sts.
Row 2 (WS): Purl all sts.
Rep Rows 1-2 for pattern.
St st in the round: Knit every rnd.

Garter Stitch (in the round over any number of sts)
Rnd 1: Purl all sts.
Rnd 2: Knit all sts.
Rep Rnds 1-2 for pattern.
Garter Stitch flat: Knit every row.
(One Garter ridge is comprised of two rows/rnds.)

1x1 Rib (flat or in the round, over an even number of sts)
Row/Rnd 1: (K1, P1) to end of row/rnd.
Rep Row/Rnd 1 for pattern.

2x2 Rib (flat over a multiple of 4 sts plus 2)
Row 1 (RS): K2, (P2, K2) to end of row.
Row 2 (WS): P2, (K2, P2) to end of row.
Rep Rows 1-2 for pattern.

2x2 Rib (in the round over a multiple of 4 sts)
Rnd 1: (K2, P2) to end of rnd.
Rep Rnd 1 for pattern.

Magic Loop Technique
A technique using one long circular needle to knit in the round around a small circumference. A tutorial can be found at https://tutorials.knitpicks.com/wptutorials/magic-loop.

Knitting in the Round with Two Circular Needles
A technique using two long circulars to knit around a small circumference. A tutorial can be found at https://tutorials.knitpicks.com/knitting-in-the-round-with-2-circular-needles.

Backward Loop Cast On
A simple, all-purpose cast on that can be worked mid-row. Also called Loop, Single, or E-Wrap Cast On. A tutorial can be found at https://tutorials.knitpicks.com/loop-cast-on.

Long Tail Cast On
Fast and neat once you get the hang of it. Also referred to as the Slingshot Cast On. A tutorial can be found at https://tutorials.knitpicks.com/long-tail-cast-on.

Cabled Cast On
A strong and nice looking basic cast on that can be worked mid-project. A tutorial can be found at https://tutorials.knitpicks.com/cabled-cast-on.

3-Needle Bind Off
Used to easily seam two rows of live stitches together. A tutorial can be found at https://tutorials.knitpicks.com/3-needle-bind-off.

Abbreviations

approx	approximately	KFB	knit into front and back of stitch	PSSO	pass slipped stitch over	SSP	slip, slip, purl these 2 stitches together through back loop
BO	bind off	K-wise	knit-wise	PU	pick up	SSSK	slip, slip, slip, knit these 3 stitches together (like SSK)
BOR	beginning of round	LH	left hand	P-wise	purl-wise		
CN	cable needle	M	marker	rep	repeat		
C (1, 2…)	color (1, 2…)	M1	make 1 stitch	Rev St st	reverse stockinette stitch	St st	stockinette stitch (see above)
CC	contrast color	M1L	make 1 left-leaning stitch (see above)	RH	right hand	st(s)	stitch(es)
CDD	centered double decrease (see above)	M1R	make 1 right-leaning stitch (see above)	rnd(s)	round(s)	TBL	through back loop
				RS	right side	TFL	through front loop
CO	cast on	MC	main color	Sk	skip	tog	together
cont	continue	P	purl	SK2P	slip 1, knit 2 together, pass slipped stitch over	W&T	wrap & turn (for short rows; see next pg)
dec(s)	decrease(es)	P2tog	purl 2 stitches together				
DPN(s)	double pointed needle(s)	P3tog	purl 3 stitches together	SKP	slip, knit, pass slipped stitch over		
inc(s)	increase(s)			Sl	slip (see above)	WE	work even
K	knit	PM	place marker	SM	slip marker	WS	wrong side
K2tog	knit 2 stitches together	PFB	purl into front and back of stitch	SSK	slip, slip, knit these 2 stitches together (see above)	WYIB	with yarn in back
						WYIF	with yarn in front
K3tog	knit 3 stitches together					YO	yarn over

Cabling Without a Cable Needle

A tutorial can be found at https://tutorials.knitpicks.com/learn-to-cable-without-a-cable-needle.

Felted Join (to splice yarn)

One method for joining a new length of yarn to the end of one that is already being used. A tutorial can be found at https://tutorials.knitpicks.com/felted-join.

Mattress Stitch

A neat, invisible seaming method that uses the bars between the first and second stitches on the edges. A tutorial can be found at https://tutorials.knitpicks.com/mattress-stitch.

Provisional Cast On (crochet method)

Used to cast on stitches that are also a row of live stitches, so they can be put onto a needle and used later.
Directions: Using a crochet hook, make a slipknot, then hold knitting needle in left hand, hook in right. With yarn in back of needle, work a chain st by pulling yarn over needle and through chain st. Move yarn back to behind needle, and rep for the number of sts required. Chain a few more sts off the needle, then break yarn and pull end through last chain. (CO sts may be incorrectly mounted; if so, work into backs of these sts.) To unravel later (when sts need to be picked up), pull chain end out; chain should unravel, leaving live sts. A video tutorial can be found at https://tutorials.knitpicks.com/crocheted-provisional-cast-on.

Provisional Cast On (crochet chain method)

Same result as the crochet method above, but worked differently, so you may prefer one or the other.
Directions: With a crochet hook, use scrap yarn to make a slipknot and chain the number of sts to be cast on, plus a few extra sts. Insert tip of knitting needle into first bump of crochet chain. Wrap project yarn around needle as if to knit, and pull yarn through crochet chain, forming first st. Rep this process until you have cast on the correct number of sts. To unravel later (when sts need to be picked up), pull chain out, leaving live sts. A photo tutorial can be found at https://tutorials.knitpicks.com/crocheted-provisional-cast-on.

Judy's Magic Cast On

This method creates stitches coming out in opposite directions from a seamless center line, perfect for starting toe-up socks.
Directions: Make a slipknot and place loop around one of the two needles; anchor loop counts as first st. Hold needles tog, with needle that yarn is attached to on top. In other hand, hold yarn so tail goes over index finger and yarn attached to ball goes over thumb. Bring tip of bottom needle over strand of yarn on finger (top strand), around and under yarn and back up, making a loop around needle. Pull loop snug. Bring top needle (with slipknot) over yarn tail on thumb (bottom strand), around and under yarn and back up, making a loop around needle. Pull loop snug. Cont casting on sts until desired number is reached; top yarn strand always wraps around bottom needle, and bottom yarn strand always wraps around top needle. A tutorial can be found at https://tutorials.knitpicks.com/judys-magic-cast-on.

Stretchy Bind Off

Directions: K2, *insert LH needle into front of 2 sts on RH needle and knit them tog—1 st remains on RH needle. K1; rep from * until all sts have been bound off. A tutorial can be found at https://tutorials.knitpicks.com/go-your-own-way-socks-toe-up-part-7-binding-off.

Jeny's Surprisingly Stretchy Bind Off (for 1x1 Rib)

Directions: Reverse YO, K1, pass YO over; *YO, P1, pass YO and previous st over P1; reverse YO, K1, pass YO and previous st over K1; rep from * until 1 st is left, then break working yarn and pull it through final st to complete BO.

Kitchener Stitch (also called Grafting)

Seamlessly join two sets of live stitches together.
Directions: With an equal number of sts on two needles, break yarn leaving a tail approx four times as long as the row of sts, and thread through a blunt yarn needle. Hold needles parallel with WSs facing in and both needles pointing to the right. Perform Step 2 on the first front st, then Step 4 on the first back st, then continue from Step 1, always pulling yarn tightly so the grafted row tension matches the knitted fabric:
Step 1: Pull yarn needle K-wise through front st and drop st from knitting needle.
Step 2: Pull yarn needle P-wise through next front st, leaving st on knitting needle.
Step 3: Pull yarn needle P-wise through first back st and drop st from knitting needle.
Step 4: Pull yarn needle K-wise through next back st, leaving st on knitting needle.
Rep Steps 1-4 until all sts have been grafted together, finishing by working Step 1 through the last remaining front st, then Step 3 through the last remaining back st. A tutorial can be found at https://tutorials.knitpicks.com/kitchener-stitch.

Short Rows

There are several options for how to handle short rows, so you may see different suggestions/intructions in a pattern.

Wrap and Turn (W&T) (one option for Short Rows)

Work until the st to be wrapped. If knitting: Bring yarn to front, Sl next st P-wise, return yarn to back; turn work, and Sl wrapped st onto RH needle. Cont across row. If purling: Bring yarn to back of work, Sl next st P-wise, return yarn to front; turn work and Sl wrapped st onto RH needle. Cont across row.
Picking up Wraps: Work to wrapped st. If knitting: Insert RH needle under wrap, then through wrapped st K-wise; K st and wrap tog. If purling: Sl wrapped st P-wise onto RH needle, use LH needle to lift wrap and place it onto RH needle; Sl wrap and st back onto LH needle, and P tog.
A tutorial for W&T can be found at https://tutorials.knitpicks.com/short-rows-wrap-and-turn-or-wt.

German Short Rows (another option for Short Rows)

Work to turning point; turn. WYIF, Sl first st P-wise. Bring yarn over back of right needle, pulling firmly to create a "double stitch" on RH needle. If next st is a K st, leave yarn at back; if next st is a P st, bring yarn to front between needles. When it's time to work into double st, knit both strands tog.

Cream 23730	Merlot Hthr. 24014	Coriander Hthr. 25544	Bouquet Hthr. 25091	Hyacinth 23721	Opal Hthr. 24559
White 23728	Autumn Hthr. 24002	Oregon Coast Hthr. 25541	Ice Lily 25999	Pennyroyal 25090	Sagebrush 25549
Mist 23733	Rooibos Hthr. 25551	Camel Hthr. 24241	Seraphim 26037	Haze Hthr. 26041	Clarity 25548
Finnley Hthr. 26043	Hazelnut 24563	Oyster Hthr. 24559	Iris Hthr. 24012	Aster 24576	Wonderland H 26044
Silver 24586	Brown Sugar 25994	Almond 24560	Mineral Hthr. 25546	French Lavender 24575	Caribbean 25095
Marble Hthr. 24244	Toffee 25995	Wheat Hthr. 26056	Urchin 26038	Majestic 24574	Cyan 24583
Ash 23731	Brindle Hthr. 24004	Doe 24240	Comfrey 26050	Blue Note Hthr. 24011	Whirlpool 24579
Gosling 26052	Clove Hthr. 25538	Mongoose 25084	Clematis Hthr. 24013	Ciel 26045	Sky 23724
Hare Hthr. 26042	Wallaby 24561	Briar Hthr. 26058	Stellar Hthr. 26053	Bluebell 24578	Pool 23723
Puma Hthr. 26059	Caper 25545	Bison 24562	Bittersweet Hthr. 24239	Chicory 24577	Blue 23722
Pumice Hthr. 25534	Sea Grass 26049	Bark 23737	Asphalt Hthr. 24243	Celestial 24582	Delta 24580
Lynx Hthr. 26058	Verdant Hthr. 24006	Grizzly Hthr. 25532	Black 23729	Jay 24581	Marine Hth 24010
	Thicket 25085		Abyss Hthr. 25993		Midnight Ht 25540
			Navy 24001		

THIS COLLECTION FEATURES **PALETTE**™

Macaw 25530	Celadon Hthr. 24254	Cornmeal 24252	Rose Hip 24556	Peony 25093	Victorian 25996
Pistachio 25550	Alfalfa 25097	Semolina 24250	Conch 24557	Tea Rose 25997	Mauve 25092
Tranquil 25094	Limeade Hthr. 25536	Canary 25531	Mai Tai Hthr. 24555	Blush 23718	Cosmopolitan 24568
...epool Hthr. 24007	Peapod 25098	Safflower 25086	Golden Hthr. 24005	Blossom Hthr. 24570	Fuchsia 24566
Seafaring 26048	Edamame 24257	Custard 24558	Kumquat Hthr. 25088	Cotton Candy 24569	Lady Slipper 24573
Marina 25547	Clover 24256	Green Tea Hthr. 24258	Sweet Potato 24259	Rouge 24567	Huckleberry Hthr. 24259
...lypso Hthr. 24009	Spearmint 24253	Tarragon 25099	Orange 24554	Lipstick 24245	Lantana 24572
Spruce 25535	Grass 24585	Lichen 26047	Cayenne 26057	Raspberry Hthr. 24247	Fairy Tale 24565
Shoal 26054	Teal 24000	Serpentine 25100	Tomato 25533	Pimento 24246	Regal 25089
...forest Hthr. 24008	Ivy 23999	Brass Hthr. 25542	Serrano 24553	Hollyberry 25539	Mulberry 24571
...rora Hthr. 25537	Forest Hthr. 24584	Turmeric 24251	Salsa Hthr. 24003	Garnet Hthr. 24015	Eggplant 24255
	Shire Hthr. 26039			Lingonberry Hthr. 25998	
...uglas Fir 26046	Larch Hthr. 25543	Suede 24242	Masala 24248	Currant 24564	Indigo Hthr. 26051

Fingering Weight 100% Peruvian Highland Wool

Knit Picks yarn is both luxe and affordable—a seeming contradiction trounced! But it's not just about the pretty colors; we also care deeply about fiber quality and fair labor practices, leaving you with a gorgeously reliable product you'll turn to time and time again.